THE FILMMAKER'S EYE:
THE LANGUAGE OF THE LENS

THE POWER OF LENSES AND THE EXPRESSIVE CINEMATIC IMAGE

D1737751

THE FILMMAKER'S EYE: THE LANGUAGE OF THE LENS

THE POWER OF LENSES AND THE EXPRESSIVE CINEMATIC IMAGE

GUSTAVO MERCADO

Routledge
Taylor & Francis Group

NEW YORK AND LONDON

Front cover image: *The Favourite* (Yorgos Lanthimos, 2018). Courtesy of AF archive / Alamy Stock Photo

First published 2019
by Routledge
52 Vanderbilt Avenue, New York, NY 10017

and by Routledge
2 Park Square, Milton Park, Abingdon, Oxon, OX14 4RN

Routledge is an imprint of the Taylor & Francis Group, an informa business

Library of Congress Cataloging-in-Publication Data

Names: Mercado, Gustavo, author
Title: The filmmaker's eye : the language of the lens : the power of lenses and the expressive cinematic image / Gustavo Mercado.
Description: London ; New York : Routledge, 2019. | Includes bibliographical references and index.
Identifiers: LCCN 2019010609| ISBN 9780367266035 (hardback : alk. paper) | ISBN 9780415821315 (pbk. : alk. paper) | ISBN 9780429446894 (e-book)
Subjects: LCSH: Cinematography. | Photographic lenses. | Motion pictures--Aesthetics. | Motion pictures--Technique.
Classification: LCC TR892 .M475 2019 | DDC 791.4301--dc23
LC record available at https://lccn.loc.gov/2019010609

ISBN: 978-0-367-26603-5 (hbk)
ISBN: 978-0-415-82131-5 (pbk)
ISBN: 978-0-429-44689-4 (ebk)

Typeset and cover design by Gustavo Mercado
Original illustrations and photographs (except where indicated) by Gustavo Mercado

Publisher's Note
This book has been prepared from camera-ready copy provided by the author

This book is dedicated with much love to my wife Yuki, whose endless patience and encouragement helped bring it into focus.

contents

acknowledgments

The Language of the Lens was an exacting project that would not exist without the kind support, generous contributions, and technical expertise of the following individuals:

My past and present team at Focal Press and at Taylor & Francis: Elinor Actipis, Dennis McGonagle, Kattie Washington, Elliana Arons, Peter Linsley, Sheni Kruger, Simon Jacobs, Stacey Carter, Siân Cahill, and the wonderful Sarah Pickles, who were endlessly supportive and patient throughout the creation of this work.

My friends and colleagues in the Film & Media Studies Department at Hunter College of the City University of New York, whose passion and dedication to studying and teaching the art and craft of film has always been a source of encouragement and inspiration: Peter Jackson, Sha Sha Feng, David Pavlosky, Renato Tonelli, Richard Barsam, Michael Gitlin, Andrew Lund, Ivone Margulies, Joe McElhaney, Robert Stanley, Tami Gold, Martin Lucas, James Roman, and Joel Zuker. I also want to acknowledge the support of Hunter College President Jennifer J. Raab, Provost Lon S. Kaufman, Dean Andrew J. Polsky, and Film & Media Studies Department Chair Kelly Anderson.

My reviewers, who were constructively critical with their feedback, and the uber-talented John Inwood and Jacqueline B. Frost, for their invaluable support.

I want to give very special thanks to my dear friend Katherine Hurbis-Cherrier at New York University, who provided me with sage advice throughout the entire writing process, and for generously sharing her encyclopedic film knowledge time after time.

I am most indebted of all to my mentor, colleague, and "brother from another mother" Mick Hurbis-Cherrier at Hunter College. He tirelessly proofread a ridiculous number of rewrites, kindly cast his filmmaker's eye over the manuscript, and suggested more than a few case studies that made it into the book. *The Language of the Lens* exists only because of his teachings, his respect and passion for film, and his example as a filmmaker.

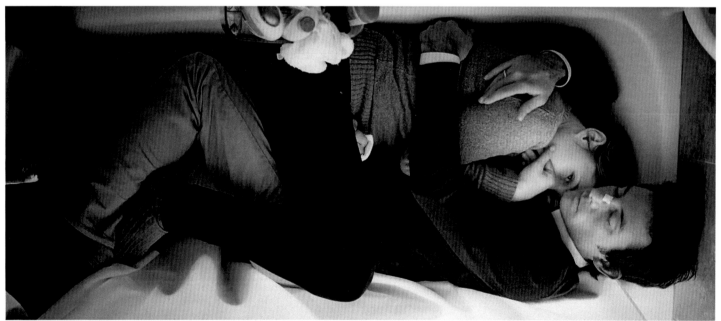

Upstream Color. *Shane Carruth, Director/Cinematographer. 2013.*

the lens revolution

In the 1990s, digital video and non-linear digital editing were introduced to the consumer market, giving a new generation of amateur and independent filmmakers a set of affordable tools that drastically lowered the costs associated with shooting and editing movies; at the time, these technologies were hailed as an important step toward the democratization of moviemaking. While it was true that this "digital video revolution", as it became known, allowed just about anyone to shoot and edit a short film or a friend's wedding with fancy "turning page" transitions and titles, there was still a world of difference between what these tools could produce and the typical commercial film. Early digital video could not match celluloid film's resolution, color rendition, dynamic range, and characteristic 24 frames per second motion blur (early digital video could only be shot at 29.97 frames per second). In the early 2000s, improvements in digital video technology ushered a new category of consumer grade cameras offering some professional features. These "prosumer", cameras were aimed at amateur filmmakers who were willing to spend a bit more for some advanced functions, like improved optics, better color rendition, and the ability to capture video at a film-like 24 progressive frames per second. Still, digital video resolution remained too low to compete with the gold standard of 35mm film stock, but the advent of high-definition video formats just a few years later vastly improved the amount of detail these cameras could capture, closing the gap significantly. In 2008, the first digital single lens reflex camera capable of recording video, Nikon's D90, ushered a new era in consumer grade video and the beginning of the "DSLR revolution"; by the time Canon's 5D Mark II came out, the first DSLR camera capable of recording "full HD" 1080p video, virtually all the major drawbacks of the digital video

format were addressed, and amateur filmmakers could, for the first time, shoot content that was more film-like than ever before. The promise of the digital video revolution had finally been delivered.

However, a critical aspect of the DSLR revolution did not receive nearly as much attention as it deserved, given the tremendous impact it has on the creation of cinematic-looking images: with the introduction of video-capable DSLRs, amateur filmmakers could finally use interchangeable lenses, just like professionals had been doing since the beginning of cinema. Before video DSLRs, most consumer and industrial grade digital video cameras came equipped with a built-in, short-range zoom lens that limited the kind of images that could be produced in terms of optical distortion, perspective compression/expansion, flares, apparent acceleration/deceleration of movement, and other effects that require the use of prime and/or specialized lenses. Additionally, since these zooms were designed for tiny camera sensors (commonly 1/3", or about the same size used in smartphones today, and roughly seven times smaller than the sensors in full-frame DSLRs), it was impractical, and in most cases simply impossible, to create images with a shallow depth of field, where only the main subject is in focus while everything else is blurry. This is due to optical limitations imposed by the physical size of the lens, which directly correlates to the size of the sensor: the smaller the lens, the deeper the depth of field it will produce, and vice versa (this is why smartphones cannot take pictures with a shallow depth of field without some kind of digital manipulation). It is difficult to overstate just how important depth of field control is for filmmakers, who rely on it for a multitude of narrative techniques (not surprisingly, the *Focus* chapter of this book

The Possession of Hannah Grace. *Diederik Van Rooijen, Director; Lennert Hillege, Cinematographer. 2018.*

has the largest number of entries). Additionally, among all of the visual characteristics that give film its cinematic look, shallow depth of field is probably the most recognizable, a telltale sign that audiences automatically associate with mainstream movies. This fundamental difference between film and digital video was practically eliminated with the ability to use interchangeable lenses ushered by the DSLR revolution.

Suddenly, amateur filmmakers could not only shoot with prime lenses, but also with macro lenses, tilt-shift lenses, and a vast collection of vintage manual focus lenses (the last largely neglected after the introduction of lenses with autofocus). Also, just like their Hollywood counterparts, they could make a long-term investment in glass, which does not become obsolete as video technology evolves. All of these advancements led to a unique moment in the history of cinema: for the first time, a non-professional filmmaker could make a movie that was virtually indistinguishable from a major Hollywood production in terms of cinematic visual standards (motion blur, depth of field, resolution, dynamic range, and color rendition). If we also take into account the proliferation of new cinema distribution platforms, the ever decreasing cost of production and postproduction software and hardware, and crowdfunding opportunities, it is undeniable it has never been easier for independent filmmakers to realize their vision. Of course these are just tools, and by themselves cannot make anyone an effective storyteller, but they do offer a technical and aesthetic level playing field. Case in point: filmmaker Shane Carruth, whose micro-budget independent sci-fi film *Primer* (2004, shot on grainy 16mm film with the help of friends and family on a budget of just $7,000) became a cult hit, was able to self-fund his much more narratively ambitious and visually lush follow-up feature film, *Upstream Color*, largely because he shot the movie using consumer grade Panasonic GH2 cameras (coupled with still photography Rokinon and Voigtlander lenses) instead of film stock, which would have exponentially increased the budget and virtually guaranteed the need for outside investment. In many ways, *Upstream Color*, a mind-bending sci-fi film about the effect a mysterious parasite has on two strangers, became the "proof of concept" that demonstrated consumer DSLRs *could* produce images with a cinematic look to rival mainstream movies. An important aspect of Carruth's cinematography in this film (he also produced, wrote, directed, acted, edited, composed the score, and designed the marketing campaign, among other duties) was his use of selective focus, possible thanks to the micro four thirds sensors of the GH2, which, although roughly 30% smaller than the Super 35 format (used in most feature films at about this time) and 70% smaller than full-frame sensors in cameras like the Canon 5D Mark II, are still about nine times larger than the sensors in early digital video cameras. According to Carruth, "all of the film's characters are disconnected from one another and affected by things at a distance. So there's a constant curiosity about where they are and what the edges around them are and what could be just past those edges. So to me, that forces a narrow depth of field. Something that's just a few centimeters deep, where your fingers might touch the edges of a wall and everything else becomes an abstract, blurred shape...because everybody is isolated."[1]

In the few years since the release of *Upstream Color*, digital video technology continues to develop at a staggering pace. High-definition video is quickly giving way to UHD, or ultra high definition (with four times the resolution of HD), and terms like "broadcast quality video" are practically obsolete when even smartphones can shoot 4K video and filmmakers like Sean Baker (whose wonderful film *Tangerine* is covered on page 177) and Steven Soderbergh are shooting feature films with them. In fact, DSLRs are quickly giving way to a new slate of consumer grade cinema cameras that incorporate their best features (sensor size, low-light sensitivity, extra resolution that allows reframing in post, interchangeable lenses) in bodies designed for video use (with dedicated buttons for video functions, filmmaking-oriented ergonomics, sensors with lower pixel densities for reduced video noise, dual native ISO technology, and recording formats with wider dynamic ranges). Mirrorless cameras (basically DSLRs that display a preview image electronically, without using a mirror) are also quickly gaining ground with independent filmmakers, because they are generally cheaper and lighter than consumer grade cinema cameras, but like them use large sensors, and their shorter flange back distance (the distance between the lens mount and the sensor) makes them compatible with a vast number of lenses. Perhaps as a sign of things to come, Sony Pictures just released the first Hollywood film shot entirely with a mirrorless camera: the Sony a7S II. *The Possession of Hannah Grace*, a horror film about a morgue worker who experiences the aftermath of an exorcism gone wrong, used several a7S II cameras paired with Hawk 65 anamorphic lenses; their low cost when compared to the kind of cinema camera a mainstream studio would normally use allowed the crew to allocate one camera per lens, saving the production the time commonly spent switching lenses when shooting with a single camera. Whether or not mirrorless cameras become the preferred tool of amateur and independent filmmakers is yet to be seen (although both Canon and Nikon have just released their own entries into the mirrorless camera market), but the format has certainly proved it has a lot of potential.

However, all of these advancements are refinements of existing video technologies, and while they are making it even easier and cheaper for filmmakers to shoot a cinematic looking movie, their impact would not be as meaningful or practical without having the ability to shoot with interchangeable lenses. Never before have there been so many options to use a such a vast variety of lenses with so many different types of video cameras. Lens adaptors exist for most still photography lens mounts, making it feasible to explore the storytelling possibilities of glass from virtually any period (an example of which can be seen on page 165), as well as for PL mounts (the industry standard for cinema lenses). There are even adaptors for fitting anamorphic projector lenses onto DSLRs, as well as special filters that can turn standard still photography lenses into anamorphic "frankenlenses", unlocking the aesthetic qualities of anamorphic cinematography (explored on page 47). Additionally, companies like Lensbaby are further expanding the lens landscape with affordable versions of specialized lenses that produce highly stylized tilt-shift, bokeh, and vignetting "creative effects" that go beyond what conventional lenses can achieve. The continuing growth of DSLR filmmaking has also prompted the biggest names in cinema lens manufacturing, including Schneider, Cooke, and Zeiss, to introduce lines especially designed for these cameras, with the same superior optics, features, and construction as their professional grade counterparts. The DSLR revolution may be coming to an end, but the lens revolution it made possible is only just beginning, making all the visual storytelling lens techniques explored in this book no longer exclusively the province of large budget commercial films, but also of nearly any filmmaker working at any budget level. As a new generation begins to explore the power of lenses to create expressive cinematic images, there was never a more exciting time to make movies.

Rumble Fish. *Francis Ford Coppola, Director; Stephen H. Burum, Cinematographer. 1983.*

a lens language

At their most basic level, lenses have only one job: to bend light so that an image can be captured. But lenses do a lot more than just bend light; they have the power to produce expressive, eloquent, and memorable images that can make us *think* and *feel*. Take a look, for instance, at the visually stunning image on the opposite page, from the last scene of director Francis Ford Coppola's *Rumble Fish*; the framing of this shot could only be accomplished thanks to the use of a long telephoto lens, needed to show a highly compressed perspective that makes the ocean in the background appear unnaturally close to the man in the foreground. The telephoto also made it possible to be very selective about what was included in the frame (the ocean, seagulls, a motorcycle, and a man) thanks to this lens' narrow field of view. The composition is clean and direct, making the meaning of the image easy to grasp: a man is getting ready to ride a motorcycle or has just arrived on one at a visually captivating destination. However, this image comes from a movie, and therefore is part of a larger narrative that makes it *cinematically* expressive, brilliantly conveying a lot more than just what it shows.

Rumble Fish tells the story of Rusty James (Matt Dillon), a troubled teen who idolizes his older brother, an aimless hoodlum known in their small Oklahoma town as "The Motorcycle Boy". After his brother is killed by a policeman while trying to release stolen goldfish into a river, Rusty rides out to the Pacific Ocean, symbolically taking over the mantle of "The Motorcycle Boy" in the process. Upon reaching the coast, however, Rusty's accomplishment does not feel like a victory but rather a failure, a dead end rather than a new beginning. Despite the aesthetic beauty of this shot, in this film it effectively visualizes the uncertainty, melancholy, and hopelessness felt by Rusty at this moment, thanks to a carefully crafted interplay of lens techniques, shot composition choices, and the narrative context they support. The compressed perspective, for instance, allowed the ocean in the background to be positioned high enough in the frame to look almost like a wall that stands in his way; Rusty may have reached his destination, but does not seem to have any opportunities for further progress. The austerity of the composition also seems to suggest a future barren of possibilities, perhaps signaling that Rusty's emotional growth and path to adulthood continues to be hindered by his urge to follow in his brother's footsteps, a point implied by the prominent placement of the motorcycle in the frame. Within the context of the film, this final image is also poignant, because it realizes Rusty's fears of abandonment and loneliness (expressed repeatedly throughout the film); at the end of his journey he is completely alone, without a hint of the crowds and human interaction that gave him respite from his dysfunctional family. As this example demonstrates, in the hands of an experienced filmmaker a lens can be an astonishingly expressive tool, capable of producing images that communicate complex ideas with many layers of meaning.

This level of cinematic expressiveness, however, requires an understanding of how the optical properties of lenses can complement the visual aspects of a shot (composition, lighting, depth of field, exposure, and use of color, among others) within a specific narrative context. When all of these factors are considered equally, lenses can help convey virtually any nuance of behavior, shade of feeling, psychological state, subtext, mood, tone, atmosphere, or abstract concept you can think of, as the examples in this book demonstrate. This approach to using lenses is what can be

Top: Midnight Cowboy. *John Schlesinger, Director; Adam Holender, Cinematographer. 1969.*
Bottom: Tootsie. *Sydney Pollack, Director; Owen Roizman, Cinematographer. 1982.*

considered the syntax of a "language of the lens" as used in filmmaking, making it possible to unlock their full expressive power.

A common mistake made by inexperienced filmmakers is selecting a particular lens for a scene attempting to recreate a technique they saw in another movie, without considering the full visual and narrative context in which it is being used. Choosing a lens this way not only greatly limits what it can express, but can also end up communicating something completely different than intended, because even when executed flawlessly, a lens technique that works brilliantly in one movie cannot simply be transposed into a different story expecting to have the same dramatic impact. How many times have you seen a shot of a character walking toward the camera in slow motion as a large fireball explodes behind them, only to roll your eyes instead of feeling awe, like the filmmakers intended? Every implementation of a lens technique in a story is unique, and results in a unique idea being communicated. Even when used in what might seem like very similar situations, the same lens technique can say two completely different things to an audience. Take a look, for instance, at the frame grabs on the opposite page, taken from two key scenes from John Schlesinger's *Midnight Cowboy* and Sydney Pollack's *Tootsie*. Both use the same lens technique to show a character walking down an impossibly crowded city street, filled with an ocean of people that seems to extend as far as the eye can see (an effect produced by placing the camera far from the action while shooting with a telephoto lens to create a compressed perspective). This lens technique, overall framing, and narrative context combination is often used to visualize that a character feels overwhelmed by their environment, commonly in

a "fish out of water" type of story; in both *Midnight Cowboy* and *Tootsie*, it is used in practically the same shot composition and setting, however, it communicates two different and diametrically opposite ideas and types of relationships between a character and a location. In *Midnight Cowboy*, Joe Buck (Jon Voight) has just arrived in New York City, eager to make a living as a male escort to wealthy women after quitting his job washing dishes in a small Texas town. The extreme perspective compression in this shot makes the pedestrians around him look like a large, uniform mass that visually overwhelms him, but Joe is still easy to spot because of his central placement within an area of sharp focus, and also because the camera was placed at a precise height to make his black cowboy hat stand out, underlining the visual contradiction between the urban setting and his country western attire (left page, top frame). Within the context of the story, this shot implies that Joe is hopelessly out of his element in the big city, and that his chances of realizing his dreams are unlikely. The same technique is used in a virtually identical shot in *Tootsie*, as Michael Dorsey (Dustin Hoffman), a competent but mercurial unemployed actor, heads to an audition for a female part dressed as a woman in a desperate attempt to land an acting job (bottom). In this shot, however, instead of making him stand out, the flattening effect visually integrates Michael with the women around him, making it difficult for the audience to notice he is not one of them at first. The effect is complemented with a deep depth of field that shows him and the people around him in sharp focus, letting us see that his appearance does not attract their attention as his female persona is fully revealed. Far from making him look out of place, the lens technique used in this scene suggests that he belongs in this environment, and that his strategy to get the part might be successful after all. Although both of these examples share a virtually identical shot composition, similar situation (a character navigates through an unfamiliar location), and lens technique implementation, they are expressing vastly different ideas. They are also conveying several additional meanings because of their narrative context, in the same way the example from *Rumble Fish* communicated a lot more than "man getting ready to ride a motorcycle". *Midnight Cowboy*'s shot also visualizes Joe's isolation, hopelessness, and even his obliviousness. Likewise, *Tootsie*'s image also communicates Michael's desperation, boldness, and determination.

The filmmakers were able to achieve this level of expressiveness because they fine tuned every aspect of their shots to complement the effect produced by the lens technique they used and vice versa; they did not aim to simply recreate the visual trope of using a telephoto lens to make a street seem more crowded than it really was. One could say they used the lens technique as a *vessel* to carry the meanings they wanted to communicate, and not as a *mold* that can only output the same idea over and over. I explored a similar concept in my book *The Filmmaker's Eye: Learning and Breaking the Rules of Cinematic Composition*, where for every framing convention analyzed, an example of an unorthodox implementation was also included, showing, for instance, that a high-angle shot can suggest strength instead of weakness, or that a close-up can conceal emotions instead of showcasing them. Like lens techniques, the conventions of cinematic composition are not inextricably linked to any one situation or meaning, and when used appropriately (by considering the specific narrative context and every visual element of a shot), they can communicate any idea you want, regardless of how they are typically used in other movies.

Trying to recycle the way a lens was used elsewhere can also be very limiting. For instance, let us say you wanted to use a long telephoto lens for one of your scenes because you saw how brilliantly it was used to convey the idea of "closeness" between two characters in another movie. However, when you try to set up the same shot at your location, you find that there is not enough room to set the camera where it needs to be for that lens technique to work. You end up using a wide-angle lens instead to get the shot, and a key moment of your movie now features a generic image that has nothing particularly meaningful to say about your characters, the core ideas of your story, or anything else. But what if you could use a different lens technique that does not require a long telephoto lens to communicate "closeness"? You could, for instance, use a technique that uses selective focus instead ("attraction", page 101), or one that uses lens flares ("attachment", page 149), or one that relies on a sudden shift in focal length combined with specific shot composition choices ("connection", page 65). Since each of these options uses a different type of lens, you would no longer be forced to give up the idea you wanted to communicate in that key moment of your scene; instead, you would have different ways to express it depending on the lens you choose, whichever it may be. Does this mean all you need to do is learn a large number of lens techniques so you can have one at the ready depending on the logistics of your location and the lens you end up using? Of course not. As we saw in the examples from *Midnight Cowboy* and *Tootsie*, lens techniques are not interchangeable; you cannot "plug and play" them.

A better approach is to select a lens based on one or more of the fundamental visual aspects it can control (space, movement, focus, flares, distortion, and "intangible qualities"– the optical characteristics that are unique to each lens), after considering how they can best support the context of your story and framing of your shots. Any lens, regardless of its focal length, quality, type, speed, or construction, lets you have a measure of control over these basic visual aspects, giving you a lot of possibilities to create expressive images whether you are shooting with state-of-the-art cinema glass or a smartphone. This is why this book is not organized by lens type or by lens technique, but by the visual aspect a lens can manipulate. You could check out the *Focus* chapter, for instance, to find a number of examples where focus techniques that use a variety of lenses to communicate a wide range of ideas are analyzed to explain not just *how* they work with each particular shot composition, but also *why* they work within the specific narrative context they support. The aim of these case studies is not to provide you with lens technique "recipes", but with lens technique *principles* that you can adapt to the unique circumstances of your movie. Since a basic understanding of the optical properties of lenses is necessary to use them in a more informed manner, a *Technical Concepts* chapter includes brief summaries and term definitions to get you started, but for a more comprehensive view of these and many other concepts, I highly recommend a book I illustrated for my mentor and colleague Mick Hurbis-Cherrier: *Voice & Vision: A Creative Approach to Narrative Filmmaking*, 3rd edition (also published by Taylor & Francis). In more ways than I can list here, both *The Language of the Lens* and *The Filmmaker's Eye* were inspired by the integrated approach *Voice & Vision* uses to cover every

technical, aesthetic, narrative, and logistical aspect of film and video preproduction, production, and postproduction to develop the creative vision of a filmmaker. As you go through the pages of this book and discover the brilliant ways master filmmakers have harnessed the power of lenses to create compelling images, I hope their example inspires you to eventually develop your own "language of the lens" to tell your stories. Now what are you waiting for? Get some glass on that camera!

a

b

Elizabeth. *Shekhar Kapur, Director; Remi Adefarasin, Cinematographer. 1998.*

lenses & image systems

Film is the only art form that uses a sequence of moving images to tell stories. This has profound implications on how an audience interprets what they see in a movie, because when an image is shown as part of a narrative that involves other images, it communicates meanings that go beyond what it can convey by itself (as demonstrated by the example from *Rumble Fish* in the previous chapter). When a shot appears on screen, its composition, lighting, art direction, depth of field – everything that can be seen and heard – communicates an idea; but when another shot is added, it will affect how *both* images are understood. The combination of their individual meanings will produce a third meaning, created by the viewer through a mental process we still do not fully understand. Lev Kuleshov, a Russian filmmaker, theorist, and founder of the Moscow Film School, first analyzed this effect with a famous experiment that demonstrated what is now known as the *Kuleshov Effect*. The experiment (details of which are mostly anecdotal) involved showing his students a shot of a girl in a coffin followed by a close-up of a man with a neutral expression on his face, and then a shot of a bowl of soup followed by the same close-up of the man he had used previously, and finally a shot of a little girl followed again by the same shot of the man. Kuleshov's students praised the man's ability to convey sadness, hunger, and joy respectively, ignorant of the fact that the same image of the man had been reused between the shots of the coffin, the soup, and the little girl. The *Kuleshov Effect* shows that the juxtaposition of shots produces an additional meaning that is not contained in each individual shot. In a feature film, this effect takes a much more complex form, because the larger number of shots involved (the average feature film contains between 1,000 and 2,000 shots depending on the genre) re-

sults in images affecting not just the meaning of contiguous images, but also of images at other points in the story. All of the images in a film inform, contextualize, and add to their collective meaning in a way that is unique to every story, because the context of every story is unique and is told using a unique combination of images. This explains how the same visual trope of showing a character walking down a crowded city street (examined in the previous chapter) can effectively communicate completely different ideas in *Midnight Cowboy* and *Tootsie*: in each movie, the accumulation of images shape its meaning differently, in the same way the shot of the bowl of soup made Kuleshov's students think the man looked hungry. This unique interaction of images therefore functions as a system, communicating a movie's themes, core ideas, subtext, character arcs, emotions, tone, and any other attribute of its narrative. A movie's *image system* can exist by design, when filmmakers plan a visual strategy that takes into account the relationships that will inevitably happen between all the images they choose to tell their story, or by accident, when there is no forethought behind their interaction. Intended or not, image systems are an intrinsic part of the visual language of movies, and when used thoughtfully, can add layers of meaning, nuance, and depth to your stories.

Although audiences may not realize it, they are familiar with some of the ways filmmakers use image systems in movies. For instance, a well-known visual trope consists of using an image at the beginning of a story that is repeated or recreated toward the end; the opening image is usually designed to make a strong impression on a viewer, through its composition, its narrative context, or any other characteristic that may make it stand out. At some point toward the end of the movie, the same image or one that very closely resembles it is shown again; their similarity invites comparison, and their key placement within the film, at the opening and closing of the story, ensures that they will be easily recalled by the audience. The repetition of these images usually signals that the story has come full circle and the end is near; it can also function to visualize a character's arc, showcasing a change in their appearance, attitude, or way of thinking from what the audience saw at the beginning of the story. Although this visual trope is relatively easy to spot (because it is frequently used and designed to be memorable), there are countless other types of image system associations that may not be quite as noticeable, or may involve many more shots, or may work gradually, almost subliminally on an audience over the course of an entire film. Some associations may rely on other visual aspects besides shot composition; for instance, the use of a particular color could be allocated to different stages of a character's arc, or editing patterns could be adjusted to show a gradual change in pace to reflect a theme, or different styles of lighting could chart a symbolic progression in the tone of a story from light to dark (or vice versa).

Lenses, one of the primary image creation tools in a cinematographer's arsenal, can play a defining role in the implementation of an image system. A brilliant example of this can be seen in director Shekhar Kapur's *Elizabeth*, a biographical drama based on the early reign of Queen Elizabeth I of England (Cate Blanchett), as she transforms from the naive and politically inexperienced daughter of King Henry VIII into the savvy and ruthless monarch that would become the "Virgin Queen". This transformation is carefully charted through lighting, shot composition, art direction, make-up, and costume choices, but lenses play a particularly pivotal role in *Elizabeth*'s image system. Focal length, depth of field, and perspective distortion are also allocated in a structured manner to visualize her emotional and psychological growth over the course of the film.

One of the core ideas in *Elizabeth* deals with the clash between her private and public life, between her personal desires as a woman and her duties as a monarch, and her ultimate realization that they cannot be reconciled if she is to become an effective ruler. This dichotomy is visualized so consistently throughout the film that it can be seen by looking at just two images: one from the first scene that introduces Elizabeth (a), and one from the last scene of the film, where she declares her symbolic marriage to England to become the "Virgin Queen" (b). The first shot shows her dancing in a field, wearing an informal dress and minimal make-up. She is backlit in a way that separates her from the background, adding depth to the frame. The normal or slight telephoto lens used in this close-up makes her features look undistorted and even flattering, while the shallow depth of field blurs the background and makes her the focal point of the composition. The resulting image reflects her character's innocence and playfulness as well as her youthful, natural beauty as she begins her journey to the throne. The last shot of the film shows a completely different woman; she is indoors, lit in a way that flattens her features, which are further distorted by the use of a long telephoto lens that compresses perspective to such degree she looks two-dimensional, merging her with the banner in the background. Her demeanor could also not be more different; the smiling girl has given way to an older-looking woman who seems distant and unapproachable, precisely the qualities expected from a ruler with absolute power (appropriately, the motto

"Video et Taceo", or "I see and keep silent", is prominently featured behind her). The regal dress and excessive make-up are unflattering and make her look stiff and emotionless, in sharp contrast with her appearance the first time we saw her. Every single aspect of these two shots – their composition, lighting, location, costumes, and even the actor's performance – is designed to reflect the drastic changes Elizabeth undergoes as she transforms from someone with human wants and desires into an embodiment of her nation, a symbol of self-sacrifice and regal female authority.

Shallow and deep depths of field and long, normal, and wide-angle lenses are codified with specific shot compositions and lighting styles according to the emotional or psychological context they are visualizing. For instance, scenes that feature Elizabeth expressing affection rely on medium close-up shots taken with lenses within the normal focal length range and shallow depths of field, showcasing every nuance of her emotional behavior during these moments. Examples of this lens technique implementation can be seen when she shares an intimate moment (c) with Robert Dudley, the Earl of Leicester (Joseph Fiennes), a man she secretly loves, and also in a scene where, under close guard, he manages to insinuate his love for her (d). However, in moments where Elizabeth experiences distress, the same focal lengths and shallow depths of field are paired with shot compositions that give her less viewing room than cinematic conventions suggest, and place her closer to the center of the frame instead. These choices continue to foreground her emotions through the use of medium close-ups, but instead of affection or love, they visualize inner conflict and self-doubt, as seen when she dismisses her trusted advisor Sir William Cecil and issues arrest orders against a former ally she sus-

pects of plotting against her (e), and in a scene where she finds herself unprotected as an assassin prepares to strike (f). Finally, in scenes where Elizabeth is emotionally or psychologically vulnerable, the same focal lengths and tighter framings are coupled with high-angle shots (commonly used to imply weakness or ineffectiveness); this visual pattern can be seen when she learns the French defeated her armies in Scotland (g), leading to calls for her removal from power, and when she first gets the idea to model herself after the Virgin Mary (h), effectively renouncing any hope of having intimate relationships with men for the rest of her life.

Another consistent use of lens techniques involves pairing wide-angle lenses and deep depths of field with wide shots to visualize Elizabeth's ideological clashes with the church hierarchy. For instance, when Elizabeth proposes the Act of Uniformity in an attempt to bring an end to religious divisions between Catholics and Protestants (i), an extreme long shot taken with a wide-angle lens that exaggerates the chamber's size is coupled with an unbalanced shot composition that makes it look as if she is about to be engulfed by the bishops in the foreground voicing their disagreement. Likewise, during a pivotal scene with Sir Francis Walsingham (Geoffrey Rush) where she decides to become a "Virgin Queen" (j), she is shot from a low-angle with a short lens that expands perspective and frames her in an unbalanced composition. Her small size and unconventional placement are set against the focal point of the shot, a large statue of the Virgin Mary at the center of the frame; like the previous example, this image visualizes the overwhelming challenge that organized religion presents to both her personal life and her rule, by showing a noticeable scale disparity between her and the religious iconography.

c

d

e

f

g

h

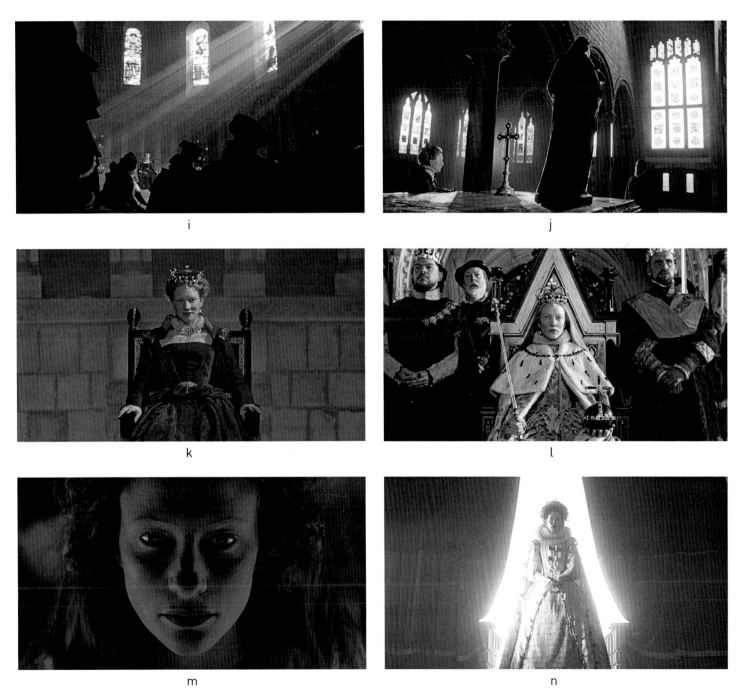

i

j

k

l

m

n

Scenes where Elizabeth behaves in a manner that is expected from royalty are allocated their own lens technique and shot composition combination; these moments use telephoto lenses that show a compressed perspective, coupled with symmetrical framings that place Elizabeth at the center of the shot. The flattening effect of the telephoto visually merges her with the background, making her look almost two-dimensional; this approach can be seen during her ascension to the throne ((l), in a shot that looks like a recreation of her famous coronation portrait), in the moments before she adopts the "Virgin Queen" persona (m), and when she makes her final appearance (n). Her demeanor in these scenes is more calculated and guarded, in contrast with the displays of emotion shown in scenes that use normal or wide-angle lenses. This correlation between demeanor and focal length is so consistently applied that at times it even reveals subtle changes in her attitude within a scene that would have been difficult to notice otherwise. For instance, when she clashes with the bishops over the Act of Uniformity (i), an extreme long shot taken with a wide-angle lens and an unbalanced composition suddenly give way to a medium shot taken with a long telephoto lens and a symmetrical composition (k) when she makes a successful argument to defend her position, displaying some of the wit and astuteness that would characterize her political style.

Lighting is also thoughtfully implemented with each of these lens techniques and shot composition combinations to reflect Elizabeth's transformation. As the story progresses and her demeanor grows increasingly emotionless, the lighting style changes, from completely motivated (by the inclusion of practical light sources in the shot) and conventional (according to three-point lighting standards) for moments shot with normal and wide-angle lenses where she displays emotion, to unmotivated and overtly stylized in scenes shot with telephoto lenses where she acts distant and disengaged. For instance, when Elizabeth shares an intimate moment with Robert Dudley (d), a strong backlight is motivated by sunlight streaming through a window behind her, and when she finds herself threatened by an assassin (f), candles in the background justify the underlighting on her face. The lighting in these scenes, while expressive of their respective narrative contexts, does not call attention to itself because it follows established cinematic lighting conventions while remaining grounded in the logic of the location. However, in the moments leading to Elizabeth's transformation into her "Virgin Queen" persona (m), unmotivated, overtly stylized lighting (candles could not logically produce this lighting effect), gives her a dreamlike, almost surreal look. Two light sources set from below at complementary angles create unflattering, strange-looking shadows across her face that also give her a "dead gaze" (her eyes lack the bright glints usually added in this type of shot), as if to signal that the "spark" of her life up to that moment is gone when she relinquishes her human self to become a symbol of the kingdom. Lighting is even more stylized in the final scene of the film, when she announces her symbolic marriage to England (n). As she makes her entrance into the throne room, the area behind her is overexposed to such a degree no visual details are present; although sunlight can be seen in the rest of the scene, it is hard to imagine how it could produce such an artificial-looking, overblown background. In both scenes, the overt stylization of the lighting is combined with symmetrical shot compositions that place Elizabeth dead center in the frame as she stares blankly into the distance, displaying no emotion. When comparing the differing lighting styles, shot compositions, depths of field, perspective renditions, and the emotional and psychological contexts of these four representative examples, a pattern emerges. Motivated and more conventional lighting helps present moments where Elizabeth expresses emotions as natural and relatable, while unmotivated and stylized lighting shows moments where she conceals her feelings as unnatural and artificial; this principle is consistent with the way lenses in the normal focal length range that do not distort perspective or facial features are used for intimate moments while wide-angle and telephoto lenses that alter perspective and the way she looks are used for scenes where she is in public view and behaves according to royal protocols.

Elizabeth's consistent and carefully designed use of lens techniques results in a highly effective image system that never fails to support the story's main focus: to chart the transformation of a young and immature girl into the confident woman that would become one of the most iconic and celebrated English monarchs of all time. The image system also adds layers of meaning to key scenes of her character arc that reveal the personal cost of her journey by externalizing her feelings during moments she cannot express them, and by visually contextualizing the power dynamics at play during the various political struggles that plagued her reign. These added meanings could not have been as narratively expressive without a thoughtful consideration of how every lens technique used would complement every aspect of this film's visual strategy.

a

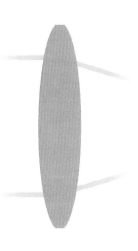

b

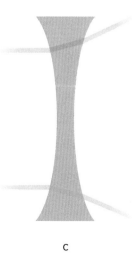

c

1

technical concepts

REFRACTION is a physical property of light that allows lenses to form an image. When light passes from one medium to another with a different optical density, it bends, or refracts, because its speed changes. This phenomenon can be seen in **figure 1**, as a laser beam is refracted twice: once when it enters and again as it exits a prism (a). The speed of light in a specific medium is measured as a *refractive index*; for instance, in a vacuum, light has a refractive index of 1, whereas light travelling through water has a refractive index of 1.3 (meaning light travels 1.3 times faster in a vacuum than in water). The refractive index of glass of the type used in the typical photography or cinema lens is about 1.5. Lenses are engineered to refract light in very specific and predictable ways; the shape of a lens is designed to bend light bouncing from a subject in three-dimensional space to project an image of it on a two-dimensional surface or *image plane* (a camera's imaging sensor) while reducing its size to fit on a given format (anything from a full-frame sensor to the tiny chip of a smartphone). This means that all lenses, no matter how expensive or technologically advanced, inherently produce distorted images, an unavoidable compromise when capturing images that will be viewed on two-dimensional media.

The most basic lens shapes are called *positive*, or *converging* lenses ((b), a *biconvex* lens), and *negative*, or *diverging* lenses ((c), a *biconcave* lens). Positive lenses focus light beams into a spot, and negative lenses spread light beams coming from a spot; since a single lens by itself cannot form a perfect image (things would look like they were shot through a cheap magnifying glass), all lenses designed for photography and filmmaking comprise an array of positive, negative, and a variety of other lenses of different shapes, thicknesses, sizes, materials, and *coatings* (chemical compounds designed to minimize reflections, improve light transmission, and control color rendition), fixed together into groups and by themselves inside a lens' barrel. For example, **figure 2** shows the internal construction of a Zeiss T2.8 21mm prime lens with 16 elements arranged into 13 groups. Even with all of these elements in place, most lenses cannot form optically flawless images, and will show imperfections called *aberrations*, generally defined as the failure of light rays to converge at one specific point on an image plane. A lens' design is primarily aimed at reducing aberrations as much as possible given cost, function, and target market considerations. In theory, it would be possible to construct a lens with minimal

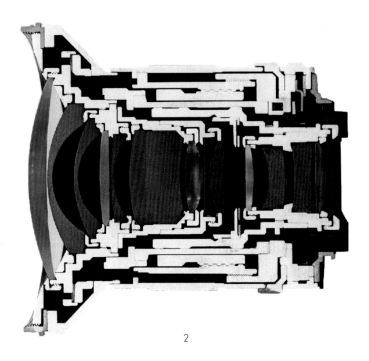

2

aberrations and optical compromises, but it would likely be extremely large and heavy, nearly impossible to mass produce, and prohibitively expensive (to get an idea of what such a lens would cost, one needs to look no further than the "box lenses" used in professional broadcasting cameras, which cost almost a quarter of a million dollars).

FOCAL LENGTH is a measurement that defines the distance between a lens' *optical center* (the point where the image formed by the lens is inverted) and the *focal point* (where the image plane is located). **Figure 3** shows the optical center of a lens (a), which may be located at different points inside the barrel depending on its design, as it flips the image of a chess knight on a camera's sensor (b). The symbol next to the sensor (c), known as the *sensor plane*, is commonly engraved on the body of most cameras to show exactly where light is converging to form an image, because in some disciplines, like film production, focus is measured manually from this point to the subject. The distance between (a) and (b), measured in millimeters, represents the *focal length* of this lens (d). All lenses include an engraving on their barrel that identifies their focal length measurement. The most

basic way to classify lenses is according to their focal length, as *normal, wide-angles*, and *telephotos*.

NORMAL LENSES show perspective in a way that approximates how human eyes see the world. In many ways, lenses are just like our eyes, which also have a focal length (considered to be approximately 22mm); since we experience sight through this focal length all of our lives, it looks normal to us. Normal focal lengths vary depending on the shooting format; for 35mm still photography, a lens with a focal length of 50mm is commonly considered normal. For Super 35 (used for most motion pictures) a 35mm lens is closer to normal, while in the Micro Four Thirds format a 25mm focal length would be considered normal. It is worth noting that "normal focal length" is a somewhat arbitrary and flexible concept, and sometimes it refers not to a single focal length but a range that can be recontextualized by a filmmaker's use (as seen in the examples from *Amélie* and *Fear and Loathing in Las Vegas* in the *Distortion* chapter).

WIDE-ANGLE LENSES have a focal length that is shorter than normal lenses; they tend to be physically smaller,

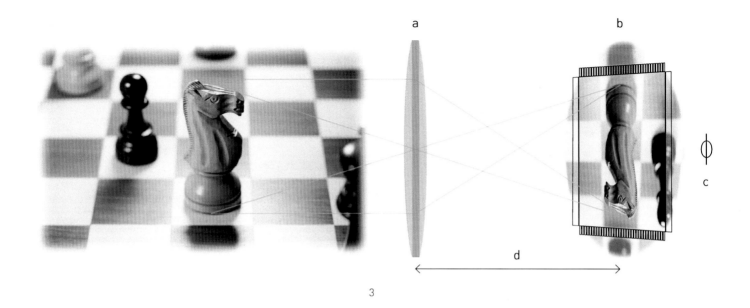

3

though this is not always the case (higher-end cinema lens kits, for instance, tend to be uniform in size regardless of their focal length). These lenses allow capturing more of a scene than normal lenses because of their wider angle of view, and show an extended perspective along the z-axis of the frame that exaggerates relative distances between subjects, making them look like they are farther apart than they really are.

TELEPHOTO LENSES have a longer focal length than normal lenses. They function essentially like telescopes, magnifying distant subjects (*tele* means "far", "at a distance" in Ancient Greek). They capture less of a scene than normal lenses because they have a narrower angle of view. They also show a compressed perspective along the z-axis, making subjects appear to be closer to one another than they really are. Telephoto lenses are usually physically longer than normal lenses, which is why they are also referred to as *long lenses*.

ANGLE OF VIEW is a measurement of how much of a scene or a subject a lens can encompass across the x, y, or diagonal axes, expressed in degrees. Wide-angle lenses, as their

name implies, have a wide-angle of view that gets wider as the focal length gets shorter, and telephoto lenses have a narrow angle of view that gets increasingly narrower with longer focal lengths. **Figure 4** shows the angles of view that can be obtained with various focal lengths in the Super 35 format. Since the angle of view of a lens is directly related to its focal length, it provides a fundamental way for filmmakers to control what can be seen in the frame. When more of a scene or a subject needs to be included in a shot, one could select shorter focal lengths to expand the angle of view, or if the shot includes unwanted visual elements, switching to lenses with longer focal lengths would allow excluding them from the shot's composition without the need to move the camera. **Figure 5** shows what happens to a shot's composition if the camera remains in the same spot and lenses with different focal lengths are used, starting with a 35mm wide-angle all the way to a 300mm telephoto lens. An important relationship between focal length and angle of view has do with the degree of magnification. When shooting a subject that occupies half of the frame and you want to reduce its size by half, you could simply switch to a lens with a focal length that is roughly half whatever you have mounted on

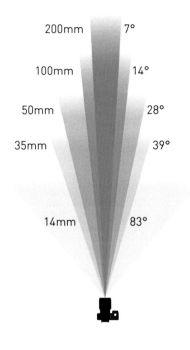

200mm	7°
100mm	14°
50mm	28°
35mm	39°
14mm	83°

4

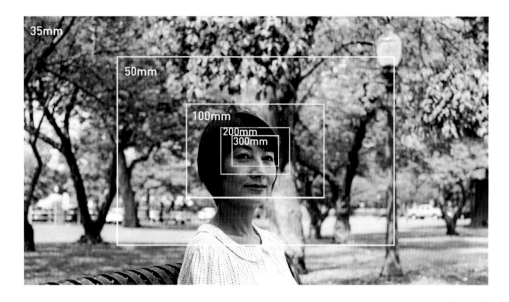

35mm
50mm
100mm
200mm
300mm

5

your camera. If you are shooting someone with a 25mm lens and need to quadruple their size in the frame, switch to a 100mm lens. While this might seem a very simple way to "dial in" the size of subjects, remember that you will also reduce or expand the view of what can be seen at the edges of the frame with every focal length change because you will also change the angle of view every time, affecting a critical aspect of the shot's composition.

FIELD OF VIEW is the measurement across the x, y, or diagonal axes a lens can cover at a given distance expressed in degrees. It has the same relationship with focal length as a lens' angle of view: shorter focal lengths have wider fields of view and longer focal lengths narrower fields of view. Field of view is often misunderstood as being analogous to angle of view; it is not. The angle of view of a lens is fixed and cannot be changed for a given focal length. The field of view, however, is flexible because it is a function of both a lens' angle of view and the camera's placement in relation to a subject. When framing a subject, if the camera is brought closer the field of view will get increasingly narrower even though the angle of view will remain unchanged. Conversely, moving the

camera away will widen the field of view without affecting the angle of view. This interaction between angle of view, field of view, and camera placement provides complete control over what is included in the frame, particularly in terms of the visual relationships it affords between a main subject and what is seen in the background. **Figure 6** shows the type of adjustments that are possible by varying the camera placement and focal length while maintaining the size of a subject constant. In the top frame, the camera was placed 13' away from the subject while using a 200mm lens, which has an angle of view of just 7 degrees. As expected, only a small portion of the background behind the subject is visible. In the bottom frame, the camera was placed only 2'2" away from the subject, but this time a 35mm lens was used, which has an angle of view of 39 degrees. In this case, a much wider view of the background ends up being included in the frame. Note that in both examples the size of the woman in the frame remained constant by compensating for the magnification of the telephoto lens and the demagnification of the wide-angle with corresponding camera placements. Another important aspect of the interplay of angle of view and field of view has to do with controlling what can be seen in the background

200mm

angle of view = 7°

13'

35mm

angle of view = 39°

2'2"

39° 7°

35mm 2'2"

200mm 13'

6

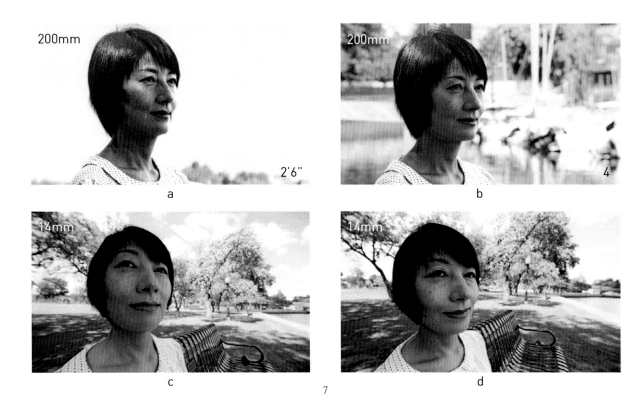

200mm · a · 2'6"

200mm · b · 4

14mm · c

14mm · d

7

of a shot. With longer focal lengths, even slight adjustments of a lens' field of view across the y-axis (by shooting from a higher or lower angle) results in drastic changes in shot composition due to their narrower angles of view. In **figure 7**, for instance, shot (a) was taken with a 200mm telephoto lens with the camera set at a height of 2'6"; at this slight low-angle, the background of the shot includes mostly the sky and some tree tops. However, by raising the camera 18" to a height of 4' (b), the slight high-angle shows a completely different background even though both the camera and the woman remained in their original positions. By contrast, the same shot taken with a 14mm wide-angle lens (from a much closer distance to match the composition of the previous shots) with the same adjustment in camera height, features nearly identical backgrounds (c, d), due to the wide angle of view of this lens. Filmmakers often use angle and field of view combinations to deliberately create meaningful visual juxtapositions between a main subject and the background, as seen in **figure 8**, in Arnaud des Pallières' *Age of Uprising: The Legend of Michael Kohlhaas*, when the titular character (Mads Mikkelsen) finds himself at a point of no return (a), and in Lynne Ramsay's *We Need to Talk About Kevin*, as Eva

(Tilda Swinton), a young mother worried her son might be autistic, tries to hide her concern during his medical examination (b).

LENS COVERAGE refers to the size of the image circle a lens can produce, which is determined by the size of the format it was designed for. Larger formats require larger lenses to provide enough coverage to fill their larger sensors. However, sometimes it is possible to use lenses with different formats, provided they require less coverage.

CROP FACTORS were introduced when DSLR cameras with sensors smaller than the "full-frame" 35mm format became available. When a lens designed for a full-frame camera is mounted on these smaller-sensor cameras, they only record a portion of the image circle it projects, effectively cropping it. The amount of the image that gets cropped depends on how much smaller than the full-frame standard of 36mm wide x 24mm high the sensor is, which depends on its format. The crop factor of a given format is expressed as a multiplier that helps visualize the difference in the field of view when a full-frame lens is mounted on a "crop sensor"

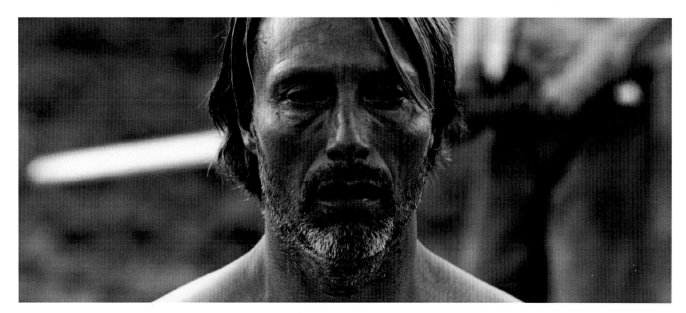

a

b

8

a: Age of Uprising: The Legend of Michael Kohlhaas. *Arnaud des Pallières, Director; Jeanne Lapoirie, Cinematographer. 2013.*
b: We Need to Talk About Kevin. *Lynne Ramsay, Director; Seamus McGarvey, Cinematographer. 2011.*

50mm
≡80mm
APS-C Canon crop factor: 1.6x

50mm
≡100mm
Micro Four Thirds crop factor: 2x

50mm
≡75mm
Nikon DX crop factor: 1.5x

50mm
≡70mm
Super 35 sensor crop factor: 1.4x

9

camera. For instance, Canon's APS-C ("Advanced Photo System – Type C") sensor has a size of only 23.6mm x 15.7mm, and a crop factor of 1.6; if a full-frame 50mm lens is used on a camera with this sensor, it will capture images equivalent to using an 80mm lens on a full-frame camera (50 x 1.6 = 80) in terms of field of view. **Figure 9** shows the equivalent focal lengths that result from mounting the same 50mm full-frame lens on cameras with the most common crop sensors. Understanding crop factors can be helpful in situations when the field of view of a particular focal length needs to be emulated. For instance, if you wanted to achieve the same field of view of a 24mm lens while shooting with a Micro Four Thirds camera (crop factor: 2x) you would get a 12mm lens (since 24 ÷ 2 = 12). Conversely, if you wanted a field of view equivalent to that of a 200mm lens while shooting with a Nikon DX camera (crop factor = 1.5) you would need a lens with a focal length close to 133mm (200 ÷ 1.5 = 133), restricting your options to either using a prime lens with an approximate focal length or setting a zoom lens as close to 133mm as possible (check the section on *primes and zooms* for an explanation of these terms). Since crop factors always reduce the field of view of full-frame lenses,

matching longer focal lengths is not an issue; however, matching very short focal lengths will present a problem and in some cases it might not be possible. For instance, matching the field of view of an 8mm full-frame ultra wide-angle lens while shooting with a Micro Four Thirds camera would require a 4mm lens, which does not exist.

THE IRIS DIAPHRAGM is an adjustable mechanism that regulates the amount of light that passes through a lens. It is composed of a number of opaque overlapping blades that can be repositioned to create an opening called the *aperture* that can vary in size. **Figure 10** shows a typical iris diaphragm set to a medium-size aperture (f/8). The size of the aperture is controlled by an *aperture ring* (also called an *f-stop ring* or a *T-stop ring* on cinema lenses), etched with f-stop settings that correspond to the various aperture sizes available in a lens. **Figure 11** shows an f-stop ring on a manual lens (a) and a cinema lens' T-stop ring (b). Most modern lenses used in still photography no longer feature f-stop rings, since aperture settings are controlled electronically through the camera instead.

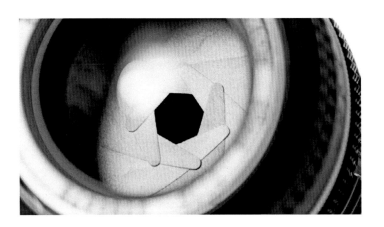

10

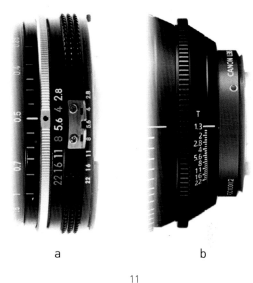

a   b

11

THE F-STOP number is a dimensionless figure obtained by dividing the focal length (where the "f" comes from) of a lens by the diameter of the aperture. For instance, a 100mm lens with an aperture diameter of 25mm would be set at f/4, since 100 ÷ 25 = 4. A 200mm lens with an aperture diameter of 50mm would also be set at f/4 (200 ÷ 50 = 4); both lenses in this case would be set at the same f-stop even though the diameter of their apertures is different. However, since the 200mm lens is roughly doubling the size of the image due to its magnification, the light it lets through covers four times the area covered by the 100mm lens, and therefore ends up letting through the same amount of light even though its aperture diameter is twice as big. The f-stop number only refers to the ratio between a given focal length and aperture diameter, and not the actual size of the aperture opening.

THE F-STOP SCALE uses a series of numbers that represent aperture settings, or f-stops, in the following standard sequence: f/1.4, f/2, f/2.8, f/4, f/5.6, f/8, f/11, f/16, f/22. The smaller the f-stop number, the larger the aperture diameter and the more light that gets through. The larger the number, the smaller the aperture diameter and the less light that

gets through. This might seem counterintuitive at first, but it is helpful to remember the numbers actually represent fractions (since they are derived from dividing a focal length by an aperture diameter), which makes it easier to grasp that larger numbers mean smaller quantities in this context (1/16 is smaller than 1/8, which is smaller than 1/4). The relationship between the settings in the f-stop scale always involves either doubling or halving the amount of light that is allowed through the lens. Switching from f/4 to f/5.6 cuts light by half, while switching from f/16 to f/11 lets in twice the amount of light. The terms *opening up* when letting through more light and *closing down* when cutting light also help avoid confusion when setting an aperture: you "close down" from f/16 to f/22, and you "open up" from f/11 to f/8 and so on. **Figure 12** shows the relationship between f-stop numbers and the physical size of their corresponding aperture openings.

THE T-STOP is a more accurate version of an f-stop used exclusively in cinema lenses. The "T" stands for *transmission* and simply means that a T-stop accounts for the light that gets absorbed or reflected before it reaches the sensor due to the optical design of a particular lens. Since f-stops only

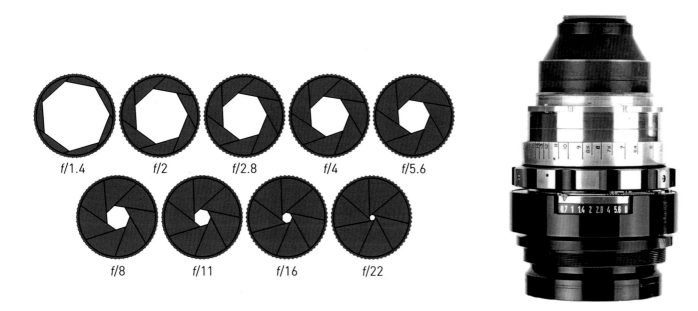

f/1.4   f/2   f/2.8   f/4   f/5.6

f/8   f/11   f/16   f/22

12

13

refer to the diameter of the aperture in relation to the focal length and not to the actual amount of light that reaches a sensor, T-stops are more accurate than f-stops for exposure control. A lens that uses T-stops is easy to spot because it will be clearly labelled with a "T" instead of an "f" on its aperture ring.

LENS SPEED refers to the light gathering performance of a lens according to its maximum aperture. A lens with a wide maximum aperture, like f/1.4, is designated as *fast*, because it would require less time to correctly expose an image at a given ISO than a *slow* lens with a smaller maximum aperture. Fast lenses require less light to register an image than slow lenses, making them extremely desirable in low-light situations. Since this is a critical aspect of a lens, the maximum aperture is always engraved somewhere on the barrel, usually in the form of a number "1" followed by a colon and the maximum aperture: "1:1.4". Zoom lenses commonly have two maximum apertures listed, one for each end of their focal length range (there are some zooms, however, that are capable of maintaining the same maximum aperture throughout their entire zoom range). For instance, a zoom

with a maximum aperture of "1:3.5–5.6" indicates that at its shortest focal length it will open up to f/3.5 (typically slow for a zoom lens) and at its longest focal length it will only open up to f/5.6. The maximum aperture of a lens is determined by its optical design: a lens with fewer elements, like a prime lens, tends to be faster than a zoom lens, which will have more elements. For both filmmakers and photographers, having a fast lens can mean the difference between getting a shot or not in some situations. For instance, **figure 13** shows the legendary Carl Zeiss Planar 50mm prime, the fastest lens ever used in the production of a motion picture, Stanley Kubrick's *Barry Lyndon*. Commissioned by NASA to take photos of the dark side of the Moon, these lenses have a mind-blowing maximum aperture of f/0.7 (letting in twice the amount of light than a lens that opens to f/1) , and made it possible for Kubrick to shoot using only candlelight (examined on page 167). **Figure 14** shows the maximum aperture markings of a fast prime lens ((a), with a maximum aperture of f/1.2) and a much slower zoom lens ((b), with a maximum aperture of f/4). Note also the focal length markings found on the barrel of all lenses, identifying the prime as an 85mm (a), and the zoom as an 11–24mm lens (b). Under the same

a

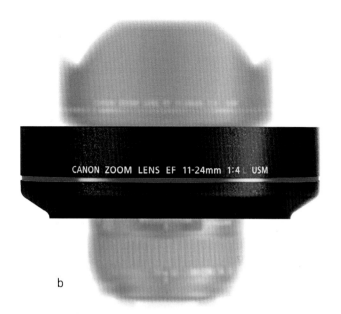

b

14

lighting conditions, this zoom would need roughly eight times more light than the prime to get the same exposure level, or if shooting with a digital camera with a native ISO of 850, an increase to ISO 6400 to make up for its slow speed, potentially introducing noise to the image.

THE SWEET SPOT of a lens refers to the f-stop setting at which it produces the highest possible image quality in terms of contrast, color rendition, sharpness, vignetting, and chromatic aberrations, among others. Lenses can register images at any f-stop if enough light is available, but they will generally produce an optically superior image when set roughly halfway along the f-stop scale. Conversely, lens image quality drops off as you approach the far reaches of the f-stop scale. In higher-quality lenses, the sweet spot is not actually a single f-stop, but a range that can include two or even three f-stops. Slower lenses can present a problem when trying to shoot at their sweet spots, since their smaller maximum apertures translate into sweet spots with very small aperture settings. For instance, a lens with a maximum aperture of $f/4$ will likely have a sweet spot of about $f/11$, which will require a lot of light to register an image, and

will also severely restrict your options for controlling depth of field. Just how important it is to shoot at a lens' sweet spot depends on many factors; although it is assumed it is always better to get the best image quality possible, there may be times when you want to purposely get an image of less than optimal quality to drive a narrative point (as examined in Andrew Dominik's *The Assassination of Jesse James by the Coward Robert Ford* on page 171), or you may want a depth of field that requires a particular f-stop setting that is outside your lens' sweet spot range. The practical difference in quality between an image taken with a lens set at its sweet spot and one taken at its widest aperture can be seen in **figure 15**. Both sets of images were taken with the same lens under the same lighting conditions, but (a) was shot at this particular lens' sweet spot, $f/5.6$, while (b) was shot using its maximum aperture, $f/1.4$. While both images look similar in quality, the cropped sections reveal that the shot taken at $f/5.6$ (c) is far sharper than the one taken at $f/1.4$ (d). The color rendition was also affected by the f-stop setting: the shot taken at $f/5.6$ (e) has more consistent colors than the one taken at $f/1.4$ (f), which clearly displays a color shift (see the section on *chromatic aberration* for an

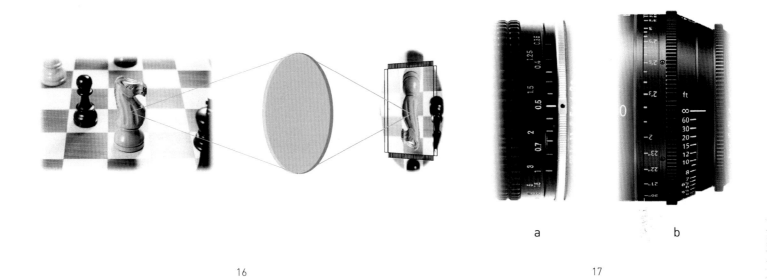

16

17

a   b

explanation of this phenomenon) that rendered the black dots on the woman's dress as bluish.

FOCUS, in optics, refers to the point where light rays coming from an object converge on a focal plane (a camera's image sensor, for instance), as shown in **figure 16**. The point where light rays converge, the *focal plane*, is critical for measuring the focusing distance to a subject, and for this reason most cameras have an engraving (shown in **figure 3**) marking its exact location. Focus is controlled by shifting an element inside the lens with a rotating *focusing ring* (**figure 17** shows the focusing ring of a still photography manual lens (a), and the focusing ring of a cinema lens with extra hash marks for added accuracy (b)), etched with various distances to set the focus according to how far a subject is from a camera (or, more accurately, from the focal plane). If a subject is 10 feet away, then setting the focusing ring to 10 feet will shift the *focus point* (also called the *plane of critical focus*) to render anything at that distance, including your subject, in acceptable focus. The term *acceptable focus* has a specific meaning in optics that refers to a standard of sharpness that varies depending on the size of the image format. This is

because lenses do not actually converge incoming light into dimensionless points, but into very small circles of light with a measurable diameter. The measurement of the largest diameter a point of light can have before it is considered to be out of focus is called the *circle of confusion*. The larger the format, the larger the diameter of its circle of confusion and vice versa. If the focusing element is not set at the correct distance to converge light rays into points of light no larger than the acceptable circle of confusion for a given format, images are considered to be out of focus. **Figure 18** shows what happens when the front element is shifted too far from the subject (a): the light rays converge somewhere in front of the sensor, resulting in a blurry image. If the front element is shifted too close to the subject (b), the light rays cannot converge on the sensor, also resulting in a blurry image.

MINIMUM FOCUSING DISTANCE is the shortest distance at which a lens is capable of producing acceptable focus. It varies depending on lens design, but generally speaking wide-angle lenses have shorter minimum focusing distances than telephotos, and vice versa. The average minimum focusing distance for most lenses is in the region of 18", except for

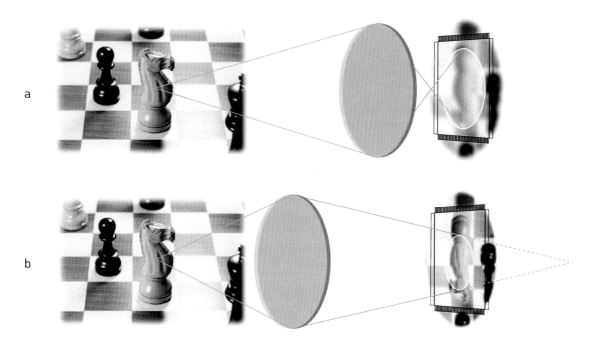

macro lenses, which have the shortest minimum focusing distance of all lenses used in still photography and cinematography.

SELECTIVE FOCUS is a technique used to direct a viewer's attention to selected areas of a frame by shifting the focus point along the z-axis to the foreground, middleground, or background. Controlling the degree of blurriness and sharpness in a shot requires manipulating the depth of field, the area in front of and behind the plane of critical focus (usually your subject) considered to be within acceptable focus. Selective focus can be an effective narrative tool to communicate a plethora of ideas, feelings, moods, and psychological states, as the case studies in this book demonstrate.

PULLING FOCUS is a lens technique that involves the adjustment of the focusing ring, and therefore shifting of the plane of critical focus, during the taking of a shot. Focus adjustments are performed by a dedicated camera crew member called the *focus puller*, whose sole job is to handle a *follow focus* attachment, a device with a geared wheel that connects to complementary gears on a lens and is rotated manually via a knob or remotely with a servo motor.

RACK FOCUS involves shifting the focus point from the foreground to the middleground or to the background and vice versa during the taking of a shot, a technique sometimes used in lieu of editing in dialogue scenes, or to "carry the gaze" of a character looking at something in a different area of the frame. The speed at which rack focusing is executed can add a palpable sense of suspense, tension, and drama to a scene, making it a popular selective focus technique when filmmakers want to underline these elements in a scene.

FOLLOW FOCUS entails shifting the plane of critical focus dynamically to keep a moving subject in sharp focus throughout the duration of a shot, or to keep a static subject in sharp focus when the camera is brought closer or moved away (for instance, during a dolly in camera move).

PARFOCAL AND VARIFOCAL LENSES define the specific focusing behavior of zoom lenses. Still photography zoom lenses are varifocal, meaning that if the focal length is

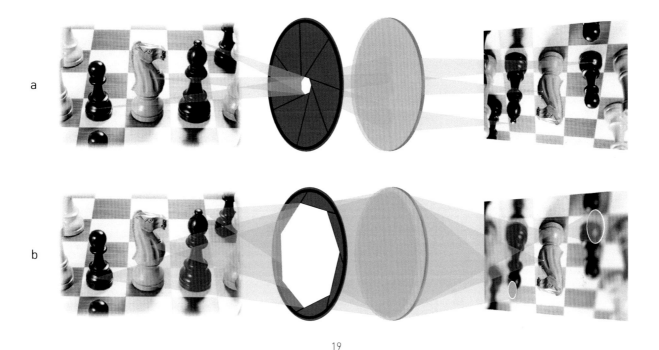

a

b

19

changed from wide-angle to telephoto or vice versa, the fo-cus setting is not maintained; it shifts and needs to be re-focused with every recomposition of the shot. This does not present a problem when shooting photographs, since you will likely refocus every time you take a shot anyway, but can be very distracting when shooting video. Varifocal lenses also change the framing of a shot every time focus is adjusted, a phenomenon known as *lens breathing*. Conversely, parfocal lenses (commonly designed for video production) maintain focus once it is set regardless of focal length changes. With a parfocal lens you can simply zoom in all the way to your subject, adjust focus, and then zoom out to any focal length you want without losing focus. Parfocal lenses also minimize lens breathing to almost imperceptible levels.

DEPTH OF FIELD (DOF) is defined as the range in front of and behind the plane of critical focus (usually your subject) perceived to be in acceptable focus according to the circle of confusion standard for the image format you are using. This range can be manipulated so it is very shallow, keeping only a small area in focus, or very deep, making almost every-thing from the foreground to the background look sharp. All

selective focus techniques rely on controlling how deep or shallow the depth of field is, making it an essential storytell-ing tool. The three main ways to manipulate depth of field are through the aperture setting, the focusing distance, and the focal length of the lens.

DOF – APERTURE SETTING is the preferred method to con-trol depth of field by filmmakers, because it does not im-pact the composition of a shot (unlike focusing distance and focal length). The smaller the aperture setting, the deeper the depth of field, and the wider the aperture setting, the shallower it becomes. **Figure 19** shows why this happens: with a small aperture (a), the light bouncing from subjects farther away and closer to the lens has to squeeze through a smaller opening, forming light cones with smaller diam-eters that are closer in size to the circle of confusion stan-dard used to gauge what is in acceptable focus. This results in a deeper area in front of and behind the plane of critical focus falling within sharp focus. On the other hand, with a wide aperture (b) the light cones will spread out much wider than the circle of confusion, and will look like large blur circles (or bokeh) as they fail to converge on the image plane

a

b

c

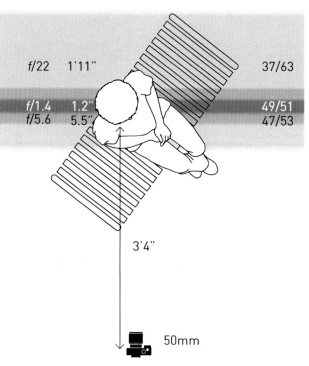

f/22   1'11"   37/63

f/1.4   1.2"   49/51
f/5.6   5.5"   47/53

3'4"

50mm

20

a

b

c

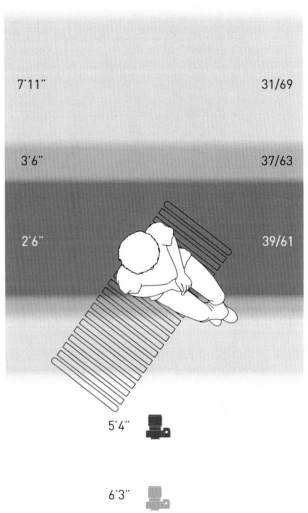

21

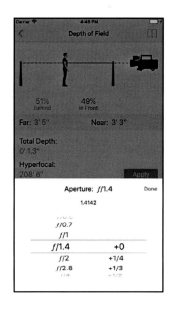 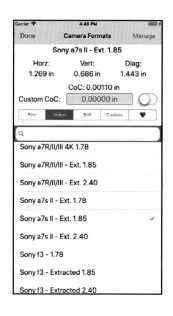 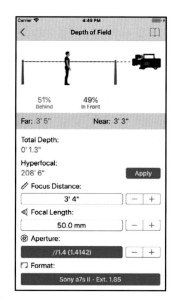

as a point, producing a shallow depth of field. The aperture setting also has an effect on the distribution of the depth of field in front and behind a subject. Wider apertures produce a shallow depth of field that is roughly 50% in front and 50% behind the focus point. As the aperture gets smaller, the distribution shifts to something closer to 40% in front and 60% behind the subject. This effect can be seen in **figure 20**, where the same medium close-up was taken with a 50mm lens from the same distance of 3´4˝ using three different f-stops: *f*/1.4 (a), *f*/5.6 (b), and *f*/22 (c). Note that at *f*/22, the smallest aperture this lens supports, the depth of field only extended a total of 1´11˝, yet the far background appears to be in focus, due to the effect explained in **figure 19**.

DOF – FOCUSING DISTANCE affects depth of field as follows: the shorter the focusing distance, the shallower it becomes, and the longer the focusing distance, the deeper it gets. Although changing the focusing distance directly affects the depth of field, moving the camera will also radically change the composition of a shot, making it a less viable option for filmmakers. Unlike aperture setting, focusing distance has less of an effect on the distribution of the depth of field in front and behind the subject, roughly maintaining a 40% in front and 60% behind ratio that only changes slightly as the focusing distance increases. **Figure 21** demonstrates the effect focusing distance has on depth of field, with three shots taken with the same 35mm lens set at *f*/5.6 from three different distances. The first shot was taken at a distance of 9´, producing a deep depth of field of almost 8´ (a). At 6´3˝, the depth of field decreased to 3´6˝ (b), and at 5´4˝ it became just 2´6˝ deep (c).

DOF – FOCAL LENGTH can affect depth of field under certain conditions. Telephoto lenses produce a shallow depth of field and wide-angles a deeper depth of field when focused at the same distance and using the same f-stop. However, if we set a telephoto and a wide-angle at different distances from a subject to keep its size constant in the frame, we find that focal length does *not* affect depth of field. **Figure 23** demonstrates this principle; the three shots on the right are crops taken from the corresponding squares in (a), taken with a telephoto lens, (b) taken with a normal lens, and (c), taken with a wide-angle lens. All lenses were set at the same *f*/5.6 aperture but were placed at different distances to keep the

f/5.6 150mm 9'1"

f/5.6 50mm 3'4"

f/5.6 14mm 12"

23

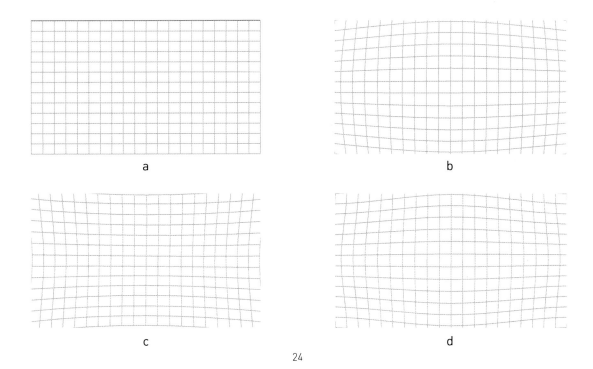

a

b

c

d

24

subject at the same size. The cropped images show that despite the difference in focal length, the level of blurriness in all three shots is identical; this is because in every example, the change in focusing distance counteracts the effect focal length has on depth of field. The much shorter focusing distance needed when using a wide-angle lens does appear to show a deeper depth of field, but this is because the expanded perspective makes it difficult to see that the background is actually as blurry as in the other images.

DOF – DEPTH OF FIELD CALCULATORS are indispensable for figuring out the precise depth of field for any combination of image format, aperture, focus setting, and focal length. All you need to do is input these values for your specific shot setup in an app like PCAM for the iPhone (shown in **figure 22**) and it will calculate your depth of field, as well as the hyperfocal distance. This allows you to make precise adjustments to increase or decrease your depth of field as needed.

DOF – HYPERFOCAL DISTANCE is the focusing distance setting that produces the deepest depth of field possible for a given lens and f-stop. When focusing a lens to the hyperfocal distance, everything from half of that distance to infinity will be in acceptable focus. Longer focal lengths have longer hyperfocal distances, and smaller apertures shorter hyperfocal distances and vice versa. Hyperfocal distance focusing is helpful in situations where you want as many things as possible in a scene to be in sharp focus, a technique used in *deep focus* cinematography and made famous in films like Orson Welles' *Citizen Kane*, Jean Renoir's *The Rules of the Game*, and William Wyler's *The Best Years of Our Lives*.

DOF – SENSOR FORMATS can limit how deep or shallow the depth of field can be: the smaller the format, the deeper the depth of field that can be obtained, and the larger the format, the shallower it can look. The reason for this is related to parameters affected by shooting with a smaller sensor, like image magnification and camera to subject distances, and not because of the sensor size itself.

OPTICAL DISTORTION refers to the bending of straight lines into curves by a lens due to its optical design; this type of lens error, or *aberration*, is also known as *curvilinear distortion*.

25

a

b

c

d

26

Different types of lenses produce different kinds of distortion, as shown in **figure 24**. An ideal lens would be capable of reproducing straight lines with no distortion whatsoever (a). Ultra wide-angle lenses (also known as *fisheye* lenses), however, exhibit *barrel distortion*, where straight lines are reproduced as curving outwards, an effect that gets more pronounced toward the edges of the frame (b). Telephoto lenses tend to have *pincushion distortion*, where straight lines curve inwards toward the center of the frame (c). Like barrel distortion, pincushion distortion becomes more noticeable toward the periphery of the frame. Some zooms and wide-angle lenses display *moustache distortion*, a combination of barrel and pincushion distortion, where straight lines bulge at the center and then curve outwards at the edges (d). Lenses designed to minimize barrel and pincushion distortion are known as *rectilinear lenses*; most video and cinema lenses are rectilinear. Although extreme optical distortion is often shunned by many filmmakers, it can offer interesting storytelling possibilities, as seen in director Yorgos Lanthimos' cynical period drama *The Favourite* (**figure 27**), which features images taken with a wide-angle rectilinear (a) and an ultra wide-angle curvilinear fisheye lens (b).

FOCAL LENGTH AND FACIAL DISTORTION are interrelated because of the distances required to frame a subject due to the magnification of a lens, and not because of optical distortion per se. **Figure 24** shows that the barrel distortion of wide-angle lenses is more pronounced toward the edges of the frame and almost nonexistent at the center. When using this lens for a close-up, its wide field of view requires placing the camera very close to a subject to fill the frame, and at this short distance both optical and z-axis perspective distortion (explained in the next section) interact to distort facial features. Conversely, shooting a close-up with a telephoto forces the camera to be placed far from a subject to counteract its magnification, but the flattening of facial features in this case is not caused by the lens' optical distortion but by the compression of depth perspective. **Figure 25** shows the various distances required to shoot a medium close-up of a subject with focal lengths ranging from a 14mm wide-angle lens to a 300mm telephoto. As expected, the wide-angle required a distance of only 12" to fill the frame, which allowed z-axis perspective distortion and this lens' barrel distortion to alter the woman's features. At almost 19', however, the 300mm telephoto appears to have

a

b

27

The Favourite. *Yorgos Lanthimos, Director; Robbie Ryan, Cinematographer. 2018.*

150mm

9'

a

35mm

2'

b

28

flattened her features because of the increased distance. **Figure 26** confirms this is the case by showing what happens when a wide-angle lens (a) is used from the same distance as a telephoto (d); if we magnify a section of the wide-angle lens image to match the framing of the telephoto (c), we can see that they are identical in terms of facial distortion. If we bring the 14mm lens closer to match subject sizes (b), once again her features look distorted because of the interaction of optical and z-axis perspective distortion.

Z-AXIS COMPRESSION AND EXPANSION is also explained by the relationship between a focal length's magnification/demagnification of the image and the relative distance to subjects. It is often said that telephoto lenses flatten, and wide-angle lenses expand perspective along the z-axis, but in and of themselves, they do not. Instead, it is the interplay between magnification and relative distances between camera, subject, and background that produces these effects. In the case of telephotos, their extremely narrow field of view and magnification of the image require the camera to be placed farther from a subject, altering the relative distance relationships between camera, subject, and background.

Wide-angle lenses reverse this relative distance relationship because their wider field of view requires a closer distance to the subject. **Figure 26** shows this principle in action if we look at (c), a crop from a shot taken with a 14mm lens, and (d) a shot taken with a 200mm lens. In both images the perspective along the z-axis looks identical despite the different focal lengths used, because they were taken from the same distance to the subject. **Figure 28** shows how these z-axis perspective expansion and compression effects can be utilized to dramatically change the visual content in the background of a shot. In both images the subject remained in the same spot, but changing focal length from 150mm (a) to 35mm (b) required an adjustment to the camera's position from 9' to 2' to maintain the same shot size, a medium close-up. Notice how much closer the tower in the background appears to be in the telephoto shot when compared to the wide-angle shot (**figure 6** illustrates another example of this principle). The same can be said for the woman's features, where the distance between her nose and the back of her head appears closer in (a), flattening her face, and farther apart in (b), resulting in a distorted look. Understanding this phenomenon is critical to shooting precisely expressive character close-ups.

a

b

29

Focal length does not compress or expand perspective on its own; it merely reveals it or in some cases slightly exaggerates it in correlation with the camera to subject distance, and this is what should be understood every time terms like *telephoto compression* and *wide-angle perspective expansion* and others like them are used (including in this book).

COLOR BIAS refers to the tendency of some lenses to favor certain wavelengths of light over others, resulting in images that have a color cast. This bias is caused by the design and construction of a lens and its coatings, and is the reason why some lens brands are thought to have a "warm" or reddish color bias, and others a "cool" or bluish color bias (among other colors). **Figure 29** shows an extreme example of color bias with two unretouched shots taken with 50mm lenses from different brands. Shot (a) was taken with a modern still photography lens, and shot (b) was taken with a vintage lens from a brand known for having a bluish color bias, which also had a worn-out coating after decades of cleaning (one of the reasons why lenses should only be cleaned when absolutely necessary). While the color biases of most modern lenses will not be as pronounced as in this example, they are still

noticeable, especially when images taken with lenses from different brands are edited together. While it is possible to correct for differences in color bias with appropriate filtration or during the color correction stage in postproduction, it is preferable to use lenses that have *matched optics*, meaning they were designed to have identical color biases, coatings, and optical performance. This is one of the reasons filmmakers prefer to work with prime lens kits instead of mixing and matching lenses from different manufacturers (see the *cinema lenses* section for more information on this topic).

PRIME AND ZOOM are lens classifications that identify whether a lens has a single or multiple focal lengths. *Prime lenses*, also called *fixed focal length lenses*, have only one focal length; a 50mm prime lens is just that, a 50mm. *Zoom lenses*, also known as *variable focal length lenses*, offer a range of focal lengths, letting you change the angle of view to reframe a shot without moving the camera. They can accomplish this feat by incorporating moving elements that shift the optical center according to the focal length setting on a zoom ring. Zoom lenses are available in short, medium,

a   b

30

a   b

31

and long focal length ranges, expressed as *zoom ratios*. A zoom lens with a 1:10 zoom ratio, for instance, can increase its shortest focal length ten times, so if it starts at 10mm, it will go to all the way to 100mm. Their ability to change focal length comes at a price, however: they tend to be slower, larger, and heavier than primes (**figure 30** shows the size difference between a Nikon 24mm prime (a) and a Nikon 35–70mm zoom lens (b) set at a 70mm focal length (c)), and are more prone to vignetting, flares, and chromatic aberrations. Prime lenses tend to have fewer optical compromises due to their simpler design, and generally feature better contrast, sharpness, color rendition, speed, and overall image quality than zoom lenses. Filmmakers often prefer to use prime lenses because of their superior optical performance, unless the versatility and convenience of carrying only one zoom lens with a long focal length range (like an 18–300mm) outweighs the logistics of having to carry a full kit of primes or the hassle of having to physically change lenses every time a different focal length is needed for a shot. Developments in lens design and technology, however, are continually improving the performance and speed of zoom lenses, and some higher-end models can even be used interchangeably

with prime lenses, especially if they feature matched optics (like those belonging to cinema lens kits).

CINEMA LENSES are designed specifically for film production, and offer many advantages over conventional lenses. One of their most important features is that they have *matched optics*, meaning that all the lenses from the same kit will produce images with the same color bias, contrast, sharpness, flare structure, bokeh, and overall optical performance. This makes it easy to maintain consistent image characteristics when shooting with multiple lenses, and also saves time during the color correction stage in postproduction. Cinema lenses are generally fast, because they use larger elements that gather more light, but this also makes them larger and heavier than conventional lenses. **Figure 31**, for instance, shows the size difference between Canon's CN-E 50mm T1.3 cinema prime lens (a) and Canon's EF 50mm *f*/1.2 standard lens (b); both are full-frame lenses, but the cinema lens costs almost five times more and is twice as heavy. The advanced optical design of cinema lenses makes them less prone to *vignetting* (explained later in this chapter), and they are usually rectilinear, with minimal barrel

a   b

32

and pincushion distortion. They are built to withstand daily rigorous use, and are also weather sealed to keep dust and moisture out. The markings on cinema lenses feature color-coded focus and aperture rings (and focal length rings in zoom lenses) etched on both sides of the housing for ease of reading by a camera operator or a focus puller. Additionally, their aperture ring is de-clicked (without any hard stops between settings) and, like their focusing ring, features additional "in between" hash marks with T-stops rather than f-stops for added accuracy. They are also designed to have a longer *focus throw* (the amount of rotation needed to turn a lens' focusing ring measured in degrees) than still photography lenses, making it much easier to be extremely precise during rack or follow focusing.

ANAMORPHIC LENSES have a special front element that squeezes the image along the x-axis to capture a wider field of view when shooting with a traditional film format (or its digital sensor equivalent) with an aspect ratio of 1.37:1. During postproduction, the image is "de-squeezed", producing what is called a "widescreen" aspect ratio of 2.39:1. This system was adopted by Hollywood in the early 1950s

(although it was originally developed by Henri Chrétien in 1926) to attract audiences back into movie theaters after a sharp decline in attendance due to changing patterns in recreation and leisure activities. The great advantage of the anamorphic system is that it allowed a drastic change in the look of a film without the need to invest in new cameras or projectors, since the image would still be recorded on the same Super 35mm film format that had been used all along. **Figure 32** shows what an image looks like while shooting with an anamorphic lens (a) and its final form (b) after it is de-squeezed (with another anamorphic lens or digitally with a preview monitor during production or an editing program during postproduction). Anamorphic lenses are designated as "2x" (meaning they double the amount of visual information across the x-axis), used with 1.37:1 film or equivalent digital sensor (like the one in the ARRI ALEXA Plus 4:3), and "1.33x", used with cameras that have 16x9 digital sensors. Generally speaking, anamorphic lenses tend to be larger and heavier than conventional, or *spherical* lenses, produce a shallower depth of field at the same magnification, and are generally slower (making it more difficult to shoot in low-light conditions). **Figure 33** shows the considerable size

33

34

a: Sunshine. *Danny Boyle, Director; Alwin H. Küchler, Cinematographer. 2007.*
b: Captain Phillips. *Paul Greengrass, Director; Barry Ackroyd, Cinematographer. 2013.*
c: Heat. *Michael Mann, Director; Dante Spinotti, Cinematographer. 1995.*
d: Sexy Beast. *Jonathan Glazer, Director; Ivan Bird, Cinematographer. 2000.*

a

b

c

35

of two popular anamorphic lens kits: Panavision G series primes (note the curved front element responsible for the anamorphic distortion) (a), and Cooke anamorphic/i prime lenses (b). Beyond aspect ratio considerations, anamorphic lenses produce images with a distinctive look some film-makers find very alluring. Anamorphic flares feature a thin horizontal streak across most of the frame, generally bluish in color, that no other type of lens can produce. Anamorphic bokeh (*bokeh* is discussed later in this chapter) looks like vertical ovals instead of the perfect circles produced by conventional lenses. **Figure 34** includes examples of both anamorphic flares (a) next to a conventional flare (b) and anamorphic bokeh (c) alongside conventional bokeh (d). The recent popularity of the anamorphic aesthetic brought on by the DSLR revolution has prompted the introduction of alter-native methods to recreate it, ranging from clamps to at-tach anamorphic projector lenses (used to de-squeeze im-ages during the screening of an anamorphic movie) in front of conventional lenses, to anamorphic filters that replicate some but not all of the visual features of the anamorphic format.

SPECIALIZED LENSES produce images with unique visual characteristics that conventional lenses cannot reproduce. The most commonly used specialized lenses are macro lens-es and tilt-shift lenses. Macro lenses are designed to let you get extremely close to a subject while still maintaining sharp focus, making them ideal for extreme close-up work. Macro lenses are classified according to their magnification ratio; a "true" macro lens has a magnification ratio of 1:1, meaning that a subject's image will have the same size on the cam-era's sensor as in real life. At such short focusing distances, it is very difficult to keep a subject in focus because the depth of field will be extremely shallow; using small apertures can help, but the extra light needed to compensate can be dif-ficult to position because the lens is close enough to be in the way. Tilt-shift lenses have a movable front element that allows them to tilt the plane of focus from a perpendicular to a diagonal axis in relation to the camera's sensor, resulting in images where only one side of the frame is in sharp focus while the rest is blurry. The front element can also be shifted vertically, to correct for perspective distortion when shooting low-angle shots. **Figure 35** shows a true macro lens, Can-on's MP-E 65mm f/2.8 1-5x (featuring a magnification ratio

a

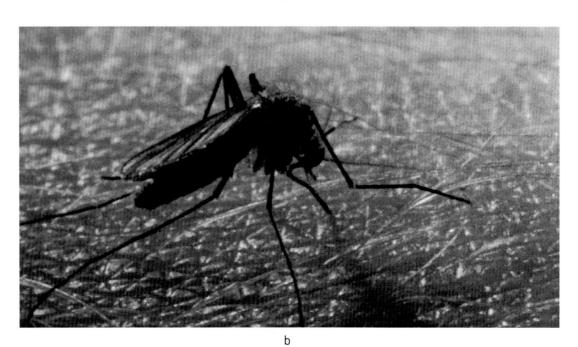

b

36

a: The Diving Bell and the Butterfly. *Julian Schnabel, Director; Janusz Kamiński, Cinematographer. 2007.*
b: Barton Fink. *Joel Coen, Ethan Coen, Directors; Roger Deakins, Cinematographer. 1991.*

a

b

of 1:1–5:1 and a minimum focusing distance of 9") (a), Canon's TS-E 24mm f/3.5L II tilt-shift lens (with a tilt function of +/- 8.5°) (b), and a Lensbaby Composer Pro 80, an affordable *tilt and swing* lens (the front element does not shift sideways like in a conventional tilt and shift lens but can swivel in any direction instead) with interchangeable optics (c). **Figure 36** shows two examples of the unique visuals possible with a tilt and swing lens and a macro lens. Director Julian Schnabel's *The Diving Bell and the Butterfly* used a Lensbaby 3GPL tilt and swing lens to emulate the visual impairment of a man who wakes up from a coma after suffering a massive stroke (a), while directors Joel and Ethan Coen used a macro lens to visualize the severe disruption caused by a mosquito to a man suffering from writer's block in *Barton Fink* (b).

BOKEH (from the Japanese *boke* for "blur") refers to the aesthetic quality of out of focus areas in the frame, which differ from lens to lens depending on the shape and number of blades in their iris and their optical design. Although bokeh aesthetics are subjective, the general opinion is that out of focus circles with less defined edges, or "creamy bokeh" is more desirable than sharply defined bokeh. **Figure 37** shows

the bokeh produced by two different lenses with the same focal length, set at the same f-stop: (a) has significantly "creamier" bokeh than (b), which has sharper, "edgier" bokeh. As the number of filmmakers shooting with still photography lenses increases, bokeh aesthetics may eventually become part of the cinematic language of movies.

VIGNETTING describes the light falloff, or darkening, that can occur toward the corners of the frame because of natural, mechanical, or optical causes. Natural vignetting is due to light rays reaching the sensor plane from different angles, and is more prevalent in wide-angle lenses; this type of vignetting can be reduced with the help of special filters that essentially even out the image by darkening the center of the frame. Mechanical vignetting is caused by external objects blocking light from reaching the lens (like matte boxes or lens hoods) and can be fixed by their removal or adjustment. Optical vignetting is a side effect of the actual design of a lens, and can be greatly reduced by closing down the aperture (or increased with wider apertures). Shorter focusing distances tend to decrease vignetting, and longer distances increase it. Another way to minimize or eliminate vignetting

altogether is by pairing lenses designed for larger formats with crop sensors. **Figure 38** shows how close the image circle is to the corners of the frame for both full-frame lenses (a) and cinema lenses (b). When a full-frame lens is used on a crop sensor (like the APS-C sensor in [a]), vignetting is virtually eliminated because of the smaller sensor size. If a cinema lens is mounted on a full-frame camera (as in [b]), vignetting is unavoidable because the smaller image circle of this lens cannot cover the entirety of a full-frame sensor.

CHROMATIC ABERRATION occurs when a lens is unable to focus all wavelengths of light to a single point on the image plane, resulting in blurring and color shifts around the edges of objects, especially in areas of high contrast. This type of aberration happens because the index of refraction of a lens element is wavelength dependent; different wavelengths of light refract at different angles (the reason we get rainbows). **Figure 39** shows how a perfect lens would bend all wavelengths of light equally to show no chromatic aberrations (a). In reality, lenses can present two types of chromatic aberration: *longitudinal*, when different wavelengths are focused at different distances from the image plane (b),

and *lateral*, when wavelengths are focused on separate areas of the image plane (c). The most common type of longitudinal chromatic aberration is known as *purple fringing*, a bluish or purplish color fringe that appears on the borders between dark and bright areas anywhere in the frame. This type of aberration can be seen in an iconic shot from Stanley Kubrick's *A Clockwork Orange* (d), around the edges of Alex's (Malcolm McDowell) derby, and to a lesser degree around his hair and hand. Longitudinal Chromatic Aberration can be minimized by closing down the aperture under certain conditions and depending on the optical design of the lens. Lateral chromatic aberration, on the other hand, only manifests itself close to the edges of the frame, and is not affected by the aperture setting. Both prime and zoom lenses can exhibit chromatic aberrations, but they tend to be more common in wide-angle and ultra wide-angle (fisheye) lenses.

a

b

c

d

39

A Clockwork Orange. *Stanley Kubrick, Director; John Alcott, Cinematographer. 1971.*

The Tree of Life. *Terrence Malick, Director; Emmanuel Lubezki, Cinematographer. 2011.*

SPACE

It is relatively simple to manipulate the spatial qualities of a location through lens choice. With the right combination of focal length and camera placement, perspective can be altered to make large spaces seem confined, small spaces look vast, and greatly extend or compress the perception of relative distances between subjects in those spaces. Focal length and camera placement, however, are only two of many factors to consider when deciding which lens is best for the spatial manipulation you are trying to achieve. The unique characteristics of the space and how they will be affected by the lens you choose are equally important, because expanding or compressing perspective will have an effect on all of the physical features of a location. Does the architecture of the space have a lot of leading lines (natural or artificial features that guide the eye to an area of the frame) that will make the compression or expansion of perspective obvious, or is it featureless, therefore requiring an extreme focal length to make any manipulation noticeable? Does the background play a vital role in the composition of the shot, and is the focal length being used including or excluding critical environmental detail? Are there characters moving in the space, and, if so, how does the focal length affect their apparent speed and their relative scale within their surrounding area? Is there enough room in the space to accommodate the camera placement your focal length choice requires for the shot size you want? In addition to understanding how to use focal length and camera placement to achieve a certain look, and beyond the mechanics and visual qualities of the shot, there is also the dramatic context to consider. How will a given focal length affect the apparent distances between characters or between a character and an important feature around them, and does the perspective manipulation reflect or contradict their dramatic relationship? How does this visual effect fit into the larger dramatic structure and image system of the film? Does it support the visual style and themes of the story? Will the space be revisited later under drastically different dramatic circumstances, and, if so, how does the current look inform or comment on it? Film tone, a dramatically consistent visual strategy, and character psychology are significant factors that must inform any decision to manipulate the sense of space.

Terrence Malick's philosophical take on the meaning of life, *The Tree of Life*, showcases a masterful use of wide-angle lenses throughout a series of key vignettes that reflect the wonder of discovering the world from a child's point of view. Both the optical distortion and the expansion of perspective these lenses can produce are used to emulate the subjectivity of early youth, with numerous low-angle shot compositions that often make adults seem larger than life. Wide-angles are also used to depict peculiar, dreamlike imagery evocative of the sometimes fuzzy, nonsensical nature of childhood memories; these moments eschew concrete narrative meaning to create a more associative, symbolic, and emotional connection with the audience, as shown in a surrealistic scene featuring a child and a grotesquely tall man (left page). The extreme wide-angle lens used greatly expands the attic's depth and height, making it look like an imposing, cavernous space that dwarfs the child sitting on the chair and exaggerates the distance and the difference in scale between him and the man. The spatial manipulation is emphasized by the numerous leading lines on the walls and ceiling, and by the tall man's looming shadow, carefully composed to fall in an area of the frame where distortion would be most noticeable.

confinement

Telephoto lenses with extra long focal lengths can show a dramatically compressed perspective, making even large, open spaces appear cramped and confined, but there are other factors that can enhance or diminish this effect; it is also important, for instance, to consider the precise camera angle, the "sweet spot", that best complements the degree of compression being used. For this reason it is essential to understand the unique visual characteristics of a location and how the focal length and camera placement will help manipulate them according to the dramatic needs of the story. A common mistake novice filmmakers make when trying to create the appearance of a flattened perspective is to automatically select the maximum level of compression available without considering the visual features of a space at all. A more effective approach is to first experiment with a range of focal lengths and camera placements to gauge the effect of various levels of perspective compression while looking for a framing that supports the narrative context. Sometimes, the difference between an expressive shot that brilliantly supports the dramatic moment and an overtly and meaninglessly stylized image might be just a tiny adjustment away.

Telephoto compression is prominently featured throughout director Yimou Zhang's *The Story of Qiu Ju*, as we follow the titular character (Li Gong), a pregnant peasant woman, on her journey to the capital of her province to ask government officials for justice after a bureaucrat attacks her husband during an argument. Her experiences in the large, overcrowded city were shot using long telephoto lenses, in many cases while carefully concealing the camera and crew from passersby, adding a documentary quality to Qiu Ju's quest for justice. While looking for a place to stay for the night, she discovers that most of the city's hotels are too expensive; finally, she arrives at the cheapest lodging in town, where she is shown what the meager accommodations look like. The shot of Qiu Ju inspecting the rooms (left page) contains a brilliant example of a shot that perfectly coordinates all of the elements involved in expressive spatial manipulation, including the physical features of the location, the camera distance and angle, thoughtful framing, an aperture setting to produce a deep depth of field, and a carefully selected focal length for the most effective degree of telephoto compression. The high degree of z-axis compression is complemented by a precise camera placement that makes the row of rooms look extremely cramped, so that when Qiu Ju is shown entering one to inspect it, the audience does not need to see what it looks like inside to get a sense of how tiny it must be. If the camera had been positioned slightly to the left or to the right, the effect would not have been as compelling, because the apparent distances between the rooms would have been expanded (making them look less cramped) or too compressed (visually merging them to the point it would be hard to make out how many there are). Likewise, the deep depth of field allows all the rooms to be seen in sharp focus, emphasizing their number and therefore how confined they must be. Only this unique focal length, camera placement, and aperture combination could produce such a narratively compelling shot given the unique features of this location.

The Good, the Bad and the Ugly, Sergio Leone, Director; Tonino Delli Colli, Cinematographer, 1966.

vastness

The extended field of view across the x and y axes and the expansion of perspective along the z-axis produced by wide-angle lenses is ideal to showcase, or even exaggerate, the vastness of a large interior or exterior space, especially landscapes. These lenses can make a dramatic statement about the scale of a location, and are therefore often used for establishing shots, sometimes coupled with a camera move that gradually reveals the full scope of a wide open space. This look can be enhanced by purposely including a visual element that provides a relative size depth cue (same-sized objects that look smaller the farther they are) and/or strong leading lines (buildings, roads, or anything else with lines that converge in a vanishing point) in the composition of the shot. Using very short focal lengths maximizes the expansion of perspective and sense of depth, but can also introduce noticeable optical distortion objects that are physically close to the camera, which can be minimized by avoiding the placement of visual elements in areas where it is most severe, mainly toward the edges of the frame. Smaller apertures and hyperfocal distance focusing to produce the deepest depth of field possible are also commonly used to maximize the amount of detail captured and to further emphasize the sense of an unending space extending before the audience.

Sergio Leone's spaghetti western masterpiece, *The Good, the Bad and the Ugly*, features several examples of wide-angle lenses used to showcase the vastness and raw natural beauty of a location, but the scene that opens the legendary final showdown between the titular characters has a particularly effective use of this type of lens. Set somewhere in the west during the American Civil War, the film follows the bounty hunter "Blondie", the mercenary "Angel Eyes", and the bandit Tuco (Eli Wallach), as they attempt to outsmart each other while searching for $200,000 in stolen Confederate gold. Blondie and Tuco form an alliance when they learn the treasure is hidden in a grave at a cemetery, and manage to get there before Angel Eyes; however, as Tuco arrives, he is dismayed to find the place is enormous and filled with what looks like thousands of makeshift graves. The cemetery's massive size is dramatically showcased in a single shot that begins with Tuco stumbling on a headstone in a medium shot (left page, top left frame), and then follows him as he makes his way down a row of graves that recede into the distance (top right) while the cámera cranes up to fully reveal the true vastness of the location in an extreme long shot (bottom). In reality, the wide-angle lens makes the cemetery appear much larger than it was (actually a set built especially for the film), effectively conveying just how challenging it will be to locate the grave in which the gold is hidden. The inclusion of a crane up move not only allows for a more dramatic reveal of the location, but also underlines its scale by letting the audience see many more graves than would have been seen if the shot had remained at ground level, from Tuco's perspective. This is a signature Sergio Leone technique that he often relied on to introduce important locations, which in this scene also functions to communicate a key narrative point leading to one of the most famous standoffs in the history of film.

DAY 1 OF DOOMED FRIENDSHIP

awkwardness

The compression and expansion of perspective created by a lens' focal length can help visualize relationship dynamics between characters, revealing emotional subtext that may or may not be shown through their demeanor or actual physical placement within the space. The technique works by treating the distance between subjects in the frame as a physical representation of how emotionally close or distant they feel toward one another; for instance, a seemingly agreeable meeting could be made to feel awkward or antagonistic by extending the space between the subjects with a wide-angle lens, and an impersonal encounter can come across as affectionate or even intimate by compressing the same space with a telephoto lens. It is even be possible to trace how a relationship grows closer and more intimate or deteriorates over the course of an entire film by gradually switching from wide-angles to telephotos or vice versa, depending on the narrative context and the meaning assigned to each type of spatial manipulation according to the image system you design. Shot composition can have a significant influence on the impact of the technique, making the intended relationship dynamic more overt or subtle by the thoughtful placement of subjects within the frame. For instance, if perspective expansion with wide-angle lenses is used to visualize discord between two characters, the already distorted distance between them could be made more obvious by purposely placing them at opposite edges of the frame; conversely, framing characters so that they are partially juxtaposed when compressing the space between them with a telephoto can suggest they are emotionally close.

A thoughtful use of this technique happens in the first act of Alfonso Gomez-Rejon's coming-of-age comedy-drama *Me and Earl and the Dying Girl*, when Greg (Thomas Mann), a teenager who enjoys making parodies of cult movies, begrudgingly agrees to meet with Rachel (Olivia Cooke), a childhood friend who was recently diagnosed with leukemia. When he visits her, it is clear neither one enjoys the other's company, but feel forced to hang out to appease Greg's parents, who compelled him to see her. The awkwardness of their encounter is visualized by the extreme expansion of perspective made possible with a 10mm wide-angle lens,[3] used to exaggerate the distance between them in two over-the-shoulder shots (left page, top right, bottom). The perspective manipulation effectively reflects the emotional distance they feel at this moment, but the impact of the spatial distortion is also magnified by the drastic change in the perceived distance between them that occurs when the shot cuts from a high-angle (top left) that establishes the layout of the bedroom and their placement in it, to the over-the-shoulder shots that revise this arrangement. This is because the composition of the high-angle shot is designed to minimize depth, and establish both characters as essentially the same size, while the over-the-shoulder shots exaggerate the distance between them, and, by placing one character close to the camera and the other far from it, create a scale distortion between them. Without the high-angle shot, the spatial discrepancy introduced in the over-the-shoulder shots would not be as jarring, nor would it so effectively express how uncomfortable these characters feel at this moment.

The King's Speech. Tom Hooper, Director; Danny Cohen, Cinematographer. 2010.

exasperation

The impact of spatial manipulation in a shot can be empha-sized or minimized not only by the focal length being used, but also by the degree to which it differs from focal lengths used in shots that precede and/or follow it. Using an extreme wide-angle lens to overtly expand perspective at a key mo-ment of a scene will not be as noticeable or meaningful if even slight wide-angles are also used in other shots within the same scene; however, suddenly shifting to a shot taken with a wide-angle lens when the rest are taken with normal or telephoto lenses can greatly augment the impact of the change in perspective. This type of spatial manipulation can overtly (with a significant change in focal length) or subtly (with a variation of only a few millimeters) reflect a change in the power dynamics between characters or the overall mood of a scene, visually underlining dramatic beats that may also be communicated through dialogue or body language.

Tom Hopper's *The King's Speech* features such a strategic use of a focal length shift (one of many used throughout this film) in a pivotal scene between Prince Albert (Colin Firth), the temperamental Duke of York with a stam-mer he cannot overcome, and his unorthodox speech thera-pist Lionel Logue (Geoffrey Rush). When the prince learns he may have to ascend to the throne after his older brother decides to marry an American woman, he frets about the ridicule his stammer will likely attract. The first two shots of this scene (left page, top frames) show the prince explain-ing his situation: "Logue, you have no idea. My brother is infatuated with a woman who's been married twice. She's asking for divorce and he's determined to marry her." This exchange is covered in a long and a medium long shot taken with telephoto lenses that compress perspective, flattening the depth of the frame. However, right before the prince ut-ters the name of his brother's lover, "Mrs. Wallis Simpson of Baltimore", a much tighter shot taken with a wide-angle lens is used (bottom). The sudden shift in focal length is jarring, not just because of the change in shot size (from a medium long shot to a medium close-up) and angle (from a profile to a frontal shot), but also because of the obvious visual dis-crepancy caused by the juxtaposition of two radically differ-ent types of spatial distortion (one that compresses and one that expands distances along the z-axis). The technique is effective because of its dramatic context and precise timing, right as the prince identifies the person he believes to be the main culprit behind his predicament. Although it was clear he was already displeased as the scene began, the extent of his anger and exasperation is fully revealed by the drastic change in the look of the scene; it is as if his perception of the world around him is suddenly and violently altered when he utters her name. Even the previously established dynam-ics of his relationship with Logue change with the shift in focal length; in the previous shots, the flattening effect of the telephoto made them look equal in size, reflecting the grow-ing bond that developed between them despite their class differences. However, the shift to a wide-angle lens and a tighter shot composition suddenly make Logue look notice-ably smaller and more distant, visualizing the rift that arises between them as Albert reminds him of their respective so-cial status.

There are several techniques that can suggest a special connection between characters before it is explicitly revealed through action or dialogue; one of them involves changing the appearance of relative distances between subjects in adjacent, otherwise similar-looking shots. The technique requires an abrupt shift in camera placement and focal length to produce an effect not unlike that of a jump cut, combined with framing, focusing, and other choices designed to make the visual discrepancy conspicuous and even jarring. For instance, the impact of switching from a shot taken with a wide-angle lens to one taken with a long telephoto can be greatly augmented if the former features a shallow depth of field while the latter has a deep depth of field, or if one follows the rule of thirds for the placement of subjects in the frame while the other one ignores it. As long as the overall composition of both shots is sufficiently similar and they are shown relatively close to each other, their differences will be easily noticed by the audience.

Stephen Frears' biopic on the rise and fall of world-class cyclist Lance Armstrong, *The Program*, includes a brilliant example of a radical change in focal length between shots combined with selective focus and framing choices that suggest a special relationship exists between a group of characters. During a press conference where Armstrong defends himself against allegations he used performance-enhancing drugs, he disparages the journalist who reported on his alleged cheating, David Walsh (Chris O'Dowd). At this moment, Walsh is shown in a medium close-up taken with a wide-angle lens that encompasses a large area of the press conference room and greatly expands distances along the z-axis, making the journalists around him look like they are sitting farther from him than they really are. The short focal length also slightly distorts Walsh's facial features, because of the short camera to subject distance required for a shot this size; the framing complements the wide-angle distortion with a canted angle that signals something is amiss, and a deep depth of field that keeps everyone in sharp focus adds to the awkwardness by showcasing their reaction to Armstrong's tirade (left page, top frame). All of these choices effectively visualize Walsh's embarrassment as well as the professional estrangement he experiences; however, when Armstrong mentions that some of Walsh's colleagues have also discredited his report, the scene cuts to a shot with a strikingly different look. Taken with a telephoto rather than a wide-angle lens, it features a compressed perspective that makes everything appear to be much closer to him, and a narrow field of view that excludes most of the conference room (bottom). This shot also features a shallow depth of field that keeps only the two men sitting behind Walsh (Chris Larkin, Mark Little) in sharp focus, in a perfectly level instead of a canted shot composition. The drastic shift in spatial relationships between these characters and overall look of the scene as Armstrong delivers this comment makes it clear the men behind Walsh are the journalists he just referenced, a connection that is confirmed in the very next scene when they inform him he was expelled from the press team covering the Tour de France under pressure from Armstrong's team.

bewilderment

When it is necessary to create images with pronounced optical distortion, wide-angle lenses tend to be used more often than telephotos; the barrel distortion effect of short focal lengths is simply more visually extreme than the pincushion distortion of long telephotos, which also have the shortcoming of requiring long distances between the camera and a subject to achieve the compression effect, making them difficult or even impossible to use in confined spaces. However, the flattening effect of long focal lengths can produce a stylized look with just as strong a visual impact as wide-angle barrel distortion, especially when featured in settings where telephotos are not commonly used, for instance while shooting a medium long or long shot in a cramped indoor location. Like other techniques that use radical shifts in focal length between shots (like the mood shift explored in the previous section), the impact of using a telephoto lens' ability to compress distances along the z-axis is enhanced when preceded and/or followed by shots taken with normal or wide-angle lenses, because their juxtaposition exaggerates the sudden change in spatial perspective.

A powerful example of this technique is used to visualize a strong emotional reaction in Andrey Zvyagintsev's first feature film, *The Return*, during a pivotal scene when two teenage brothers, Andrey (Vladimir Garin) and Ivan (Ivan Dobronravov) see their father (Konstantin Lavronenko) for the first time after an unexplained 12–year absence. The sudden reveal of the father lying on a bed (left page, bottom frame) is shown in a POV (or "point of view") shot taken with a long telephoto lens that dramatically compresses perspec-

tive and distorts his body unnaturally; this effect is heightened by its placement directly after several shots taken with a lens closer to a normal focal length (top left, right). The extreme flattening effect is also accentuated by a thoughtful mise en scène designed to maximize its visual impact, from the use of a monochromatic color palette that isolates the body within the composition, to the elevation of the camera to emphasize the foreshortening effect (if the camera had been lower, the feet would have blocked most of the body, and if it had been higher the effect would not have looked as pronounced). All of these elements are designed to visualize the boys' bewilderment at the sudden appearance of their father by presenting him in a uniquely unsettling manner, from a meticulous body posture that suggests lifelessness to the way the sheet covering him resembles a shroud (in fact a painstaking recreation of the Italian Renaissance painting *Lamentation over the Dead Christ*, by Andrea Mantegna – probably the most famous example of foreshortening in the history of art). A less obvious aspect that also contributes to the visual impact of this shot is its setting; telephoto lenses with a focal length capable of showing this degree of perspective compression have an extremely narrow field of view and therefore require long distances between the subject and the camera to frame a long shot, which normally prevents their use in confined indoor locations. Because of this, although audiences may be familiar with the effect, they would rarely have seen it applied in this type of (seemingly) small, interior setting, further enhancing the shock and strangeness of this moment.

subtext

Perspective compression and expansion can visualize the emotional subjectivity of a character's connection to their environment, revealing how the spaces they inhabit make them feel. When combined with thoughtful choices in art direction, lighting, shot composition, depth of field, and, if included, the movement and even the performance of actors, your choice of focal length can make a space feel inhospitable or inviting, claustrophobic or soothing, oppressive or liberating. This spatial manipulation can be overt, by using extreme focal lengths at either end of the spectrum, or subtle, by only slightly deviating from normal lenses so that the effect is more felt than noticed. When distorting perspective for this purpose, it is especially important to do it consistently, so that the narrative meaning of the effect is clear; for instance, if wide-angles are systematically used to convey that a character feels vulnerable in a space, then these focal lengths should be avoided when showing spaces that are supposed to feel safe. Although most audiences will not be consciously aware that spaces are being manipulated in this way (especially if the effect is subtle), they will internalize the intended psychological or emotional significance along with the visual approach.

A particularly effective application of this principle is used by director Mark Romanek in *One Hour Photo*, the story of a lonely middle aged photo lab technician, Sy Parrish (Robin Williams), who becomes pathologically obsessed with the Yorkins, a family whose pictures he develops at a supermarket. When he discovers that Will Yorkin is cheating on his wife, threatening to disrupt the idyllic family life he fantasizes they have, he decides to intervene, revealing the dark nature of his fixation. Sy spends most of his time in three environments: the supermarket where he works, his apartment, and, secretly, the Yorkins' house. According to Romanek, the spatial qualities of each of these locations were manipulated to reflect Sy's emotional connection to them, which were complemented with carefully selected art direction and lighting choices.[3] The supermarket was shot mainly with wide-angle lenses that expanded perspective and created a distorted sense of depth, suggesting a spacious, unrestricted environment that is in stark contrast with his apartment, shot with mostly telephoto lenses that flattened the depth of the frame, making it feel restrictive and oppressive. Accordingly, Sy displays a deeply emotional attachment to the supermarket, being the only place that lets him have some agency and authority despite his social ineptitude (left page, top frame); when he is shown in his apartment, however, his demeanor turns emotionless and numb (bottom left). The Yorkins' house was shot using normal lenses, avoiding the overt perspective distortion of the supermarket and his apartment; this look reflects Sy's idealized, "picture-perfect" fantasy of what their home feels like to him, complete with warm tones and lighting that makes it look cozy and inviting (bottom right). It is important to note that the emotional states implied by the use of these focal lengths are not inherent to them; using a telephoto lens to shoot a space will not necessarily convey loneliness or depression. Instead, the meaning of any technique depends on its coordination with the narrative context and the mise en scène of the shot.

apprehension

One of the most flamboyant shots that exploit a lens' ability to alter the viewers' expectations and perception of space is the dolly zoom. This shot uses a technique where the camera is moved toward or away from a subject while adjusting the zoom lens, from telephoto to wide, or vice versa, to keep their size constant in the frame. In the resulting image, the perspective of the background is compressed or expanded, even though neither the camera nor the subject appears to move. The shift in focal length and the accompanying dolly move can be performed so that the effect is gradual and subtle, or quick and obvious, depending on how noticeable it needs to be. When an extremely jarring or stylistically apparent effect is required, a lens with a high zoom ratio and enough space to dolly the camera are essential; it is also important for the background to have enough visual detail (in the form of overlapping planes or relative size depth cues, among others) to make the change in perspective more noticeable. The dollying of the camera makes it necessary to pull focus to keep the subject sharp, which can prove challenging in situations where the depth of field is shallow and the camera to subject distance is more than just a few feet. Additionally, the focal length ring must be shifted at a speed that matches the dolly's rate of movement to maintain a constant subject size throughout the duration of the shot. Because of all the factors involved, this is a time-consuming, difficult shot to accomplish; however, it can make a bold visual statement to showcase extremely emotional reactions, especially in situations where a character has an epiphany or is surprised by a particularly shocking event. Sometimes, the flashiness of the dolly zoom makes it susceptible to being overused or inappropriately used, calling too much attention to the technique itself instead of the narrative point it is visualizing; it should therefore be used sparingly and thoughtfully.

Neil Marshall, director of *The Descent*, the story of six women who get lost while exploring a cave system and fall prey to humanoid cannibals, makes clever use of the dolly zoom technique in a scene where Sarah (Shauna Macdonald) wakes up in a hospital after surviving a horrific car accident that unbeknown to her killed her daughter. As she wanders through an ominously deserted hallway calling her daughter's name, she suddenly notices the lights at the opposite end start to go out, engulfing it in a darkness that advances rapidly toward her. At this point, a dolly zoom (left page) shows her astonished reaction to this surreal event, as the hallway behind her appears to quickly recede into the distance, the result of rapidly dollying the camera towards her as the lens zooms from a telephoto to a wide-angle setting. Panicking, she tries to run away from the approaching darkness, but it quickly overtakes her; suddenly, the hallway is brightly lit again and filled with hospital workers and patients, and a friend informs Sarah her daughter died in the accident. Interestingly, since the hallway episode is understood to have been a hallucination partly prompted by her deteriorated physical state, the extreme visual stylization of the dolly zoom is narratively justified both as a physical and a psychological manifestation of the apprehension she feels at this moment, and not merely a visual flourish, inorganic to the story.

rage

Although a scene's narrative context plays a crucial role in how effectively a lens technique can communicate an idea, what happens in other scenes can also influence how it is interpreted by an audience. This is especially the case when the context of the scene in which a technique is presented is unclear or ambiguous. For instance, the dolly zoom technique is commonly employed to visualize a character's extreme physical, emotional, or psychological reaction to a specific event that happens within the scene in which it is used, in a way that a direct "cause and effect" relationship can be drawn. In the example from *The Descent* in the previous section, for instance, it was clear the character was reacting to a hallucination she (and the audience) was seeing, making the purpose of the dolly zoom clear: it visualized her fear at that moment. However, it is also possible to use a dolly zoom without including a direct cause for it within a scene, and instead letting the narrative context of events leading up to or after it provide a justification for its use. In these cases, rather than visualizing a direct reaction to something or someone, the dolly zoom can communicate a more abstract representation of a character trait, provided it is established at some point in the narrative.

An excellent example of this use of a dolly zoom can be seen in Director Jonathan Glazer's stylish neo-noir thriller *Sexy Beast*. The story follows Gal, a retired ex-convict living in Spain who is mentally and physically abused by Don (Ben Kingsley), a sociopathic gang enforcer who was ordered to recruit him for one more heist. When Gal accuses Don of being in love with his girlfriend and using the heist as an excuse

to come between them, Don explodes in a fit of anger and abruptly decides to fly back to London. In a later scene, he is shown standing in the middle of a busy boarding gate waiting area, still upset (left page). At this moment, a dolly zoom gradually makes it look as if the background gets increasingly closer to him while he remains the same size in the frame (an effect obtained by dollying the camera away while adjusting a zoom lens from a wide-angle to a telephoto setting). During the course of the dolly zoom, Don's demeanor grows visibly angrier, as if he were holding back an unbridled rage that could explode at any moment; at one point he even stares directly at the camera (middle and bottom frames), seemingly confronting the audience itself for intruding into his personal space. Nothing in this scene, however, justifies the overt stylization of the dolly zoom; Don does not interact with anyone, nor does he seem to be reacting to anything in particular around him. In the following scene he boards a plane, still set on heading back to London, but after a confrontation with a flight attendant over a cigarette gets kicked off and heads back to confront Gal again. While the lack of a clear narrative context for the use of the dolly zoom is absent in the scene that features it, the context of the scenes leading up to and following it provides it. They clearly establish his character as being prone to unpredictable mood swings, becoming verbally abusive and even violent toward everyone around him; this makes it clear that the stylization shown during the boarding gate scene must have been motivated by one of these unprovoked moments of anger, and not just an aesthetic choice by the filmmaker.

With its ability to broaden or narrow the field of view of a shot, the zoom lens' variable focal length allows you to reveal and conceal space during the progress of a take. This shift in the amount of visual information in the frame can make a strong dramatic statement about the nature of a space, or about a relationship between characters and their surrounding area. One of the reasons that zooming during a shot can be so narratively compelling is that it not only changes the field of view, but also the perceived physical qualities of a location, because of the way visual perspective is affected in real time. When space is revealed, for instance, by zooming from a telephoto to a wide-angle setting, the perspective distortion will change from compressed to deep; this effect can be extreme or subtle, depending on how high or low the lens' zoom ratio is, how much of the total range of the zoom is used, and the speed at which the shift is executed. This dynamic change in perspective can signal a shift in the tone or mood of a scene and the way characters relate to one another or to their environment, by altering the spatial, compositional, and scale relationships while preserving absolute continuity of space and time. Because of its distinctive visual qualities, zooming can easily become a distraction if overused, and should be reserved for making a dramatic statement about a particularly meaningful moment in a story.

A memorable example of this zoom technique can be seen in a touching sequence from Hal Ashby's *Harold and Maude*, the story of the unlikely romance that develops between Harold (Bud Cort), a nihilistic teenager obsessed with death, and Maude (Ruth Gordon), an octogenarian with an unusual way of looking at life. While strolling through a field of daisies, Harold tells Maude he would like to be reborn as one of them because "they are all alike", revealing how meaningless and inconsequential he believes his life is. Maude points out that there are, in fact, minute differences in all of them, telling him: "You see, Harold, I believe that much of the world's sorrow comes from people who are *this* (pointing at a flower in her hand) yet allow themselves to be treated as *that* (pointing at the field of daisies)" (left page, top left frame). As she says this, the film cuts to a wide shot that reveals they are no longer surrounded by flowers, but sitting in the midst of a military cemetery, filled with white headstones set against a field of grass that graphically matches the field of daisies they were in (top right). The field of view gradually expands as the zoom shifts from telephoto to wide-angle (bottom left), showing the devastating vastness of the cemetery and the immense loss of life it symbolizes; as this happens, the tone of the sequence changes, from an intimate exchange between kindred souls to an allegorical visualization of the somber, universal truth contained in Maude's nugget of wisdom. The thematic subtext of the shot is amplified by the distortion of perspective and greater depth achieved as the zoom reaches its maximum wide-angle setting (bottom right), making the thousands of headstones look like a uniform, nondescript pattern of identical objects without any distinctive features. Ultimately, the shot allows the audience to visually grasp Maude's point about the importance of individuality in the face of conformity with an overwhelming poignancy.

The compression of space possible with extremely long focal lengths can produce foreground/background juxtapositions that depict proximity in a way that cannot be perceived with the naked eye. This type of spatial manipulation works well in situations where, for technical, logistical, or safety reasons, foreground and background visual elements cannot be placed close to each other yet must appear as if they are. The degree of perspective compression, as well as the apparent reduction in the rate of movement along the z-axis if the shot includes a moving subject, is directly proportional to the focal length of the lens; the longer it is, the more extreme the flattening effect, but also the farther the camera will have to be from both the foreground and background subjects because of the drastically reduced field of view and greater magnification. With enough space, a long telephoto lens can make subjects separated by hundreds of feet appear to be nearly on top of one another. Not surprisingly, this technique is often used to add drama, tension, and an element of danger during key moments in chase scenes, when the aim is to show that someone or something in the background suddenly appears to be much closer than established in earlier shots, implying that they are bearing down on or about to catch up to a subject in the foreground. The effectiveness of this technique can be enhanced by using a deep depth of field that maintains both background and foreground visual elements in sharp focus simultaneously, reinforcing the illusion they are physically close to each other.

Rob Reiner's *Stand by Me*, the story of a writer who recalls a childhood journey he took with friends to find the body of a boy killed by a train, applies this technique to great effect in one of its most memorable scenes. As the boys cross a trestle bridge during their trip, Vern (Jerry O'Connell) is gripped by a fear of falling between the train ties and lags behind; however, when Gordie (Will Wheaton) spots a train coming their way (left page, top left frame) they are forced to race across to save themselves (top right). This moment is shown in a medium shot with an extremely compressed perspective that makes it look as if the train is only a few feet away from them, dramatically closer than it had been established in previous shots (bottom frame). In reality, the train was nowhere near the actors, but the extra long focal length (a 600mm telephoto lens[4]) used for this shot not only produced a convincing illusion of closeness between them, but also added tension and suspense by making it look as if the boys were hardly advancing even though they were running at full speed. The lens technique effectively creates the impression that if the boys slow down, stumble, or hesitate at all, they will surely be run over by the train, adding a palpable sense of peril to their situation. Interestingly, the spatial and motion manipulations used in this shot can also be understood as a subjective visualization of how close Gordie *felt* the train was, and therefore not a factual representation of the distances involved. Additionally, since the entire narrative is later revealed to be a piece written by an adult Gordie who is an accomplished writer, there is also the possibility that what we are seeing reflects not a faithful recollection of events, but a purposely embellished account designed to make his tale more compelling.

Ran, Akira Kurosawa, Director; Asakazu Nakai, Takao Saitô, Shôji Ueda, Cinematographers, 1985

order

Director Akira Kurosawa's films are well known for the beauty and expressiveness of his shot compositions. As a young man, he attended art school, and much of the aesthetic sense he developed in those years can be appreciated in his painterly visual style. There was, however, a significant evolution in the look of his films starting with his masterpiece *Seven Samurai* (1954), that achieved its maximum expression in his epics *Kagemusha* (1980) and *Ran* (1985). Beginning with *Seven Samurai*, Kurosawa developed a style that involved the use of multiple cameras (shooting wide and tight shots simultaneously) and mostly telephoto instead of normal or wide-angle lenses; the shift to longer focal lengths was accompanied with a varied and sophisticated visual language tailored to the optical characteristics of these lenses, intricately woven with recurring themes of his films. In this later stage of his career the telephoto lens became, for all intents and purposes, Kurosawa's version of a normal lens.

Virtually all of the techniques Kurosawa developed for the telephoto lens can be found in *Ran* (Japanese for "chaos"), his adaptation of Shakespeare's *King Lear.* Set in feudal Japan, *Ran* follows the turmoil that ensues after Lord Hidetora (Tatsuya Nakadai), an aging warlord who attained power through ruthless violence, decides to step down and divide his kingdom among his three sons, keeping his title while placing only one of them in charge. His hopes for a peaceful transition are, however, shattered when two of his sons begin scheming against him and each other for control of the clan, leading to a tragic ending that rivals *King Lear*'s in its fatalistic poignancy and drama. Throughout the film, Kurosawa uses the telephoto's flattening effect, a mostly static camera, and staging evocative of traditional Japanese theatre to effectively reflect the strict hierarchy and rigid, highly ritualized culture that ultimately drives the violent struggle for power after Hidetora's abdication. Perspective compression, for instance, is often complemented with expressive shot compositions, as seen when Hidetora announces his abdication (left page, top left frame); in this shot, the long distance required by the telephoto lens makes everyone look about the same size, preventing the use of techniques that rely on contrasting subject sizes to reveal power dynamics within the group (low/high-angles and Hitchcock's Rule, among others). Instead, hierarchical order is communicated by the placement of characters along the y-axis, with Hidetora at the top, followed by his sons, then the warlords slightly below them, and lower rank officers at the bottom of the frame. Later, when Hidetora leaves a burning castle surrounded by enemy troops (bottom left), the telephoto's flattening effect emphasizes all planes of depth simultaneously, producing painterly juxtapositions of visual elements that effectively emblematize his plight. A number of scenes also combine telephoto compression with blocking and framing that emphasizes the flatness of the image in a way that recalls a staged play, with wide shots that showcase body language evocative of the minimalist aesthetics of Japanese Noh theatre (a connection also evident in Hidetora's mask-like makeup and performance), as seen when Lady Kaede (Mieko Harada) confronts Jiro (Jinpachi Nezu), one of Hidetora's sons plotting to take over (bottom right).

symbolism

Camera placement and focal length are two of the most critical elements to consider for a well-composed shot. They are especially important in "emblematic" shots (so called due to their ability to visualize themes, subtexts, and/or core ideas of a story in a single image), where the arrangement of visual elements is meant to convey a more associative meaning rather than a literal one, because they allow precise adjustments to the size, placement, and relative proximity of everything contained in a frame. Creating the juxtaposition of visual elements is not technically complicated; it can be as simple as placing the camera so that desired areas of the foreground and background are positioned meaningfully within the frame, paired with a focal length that produces a field of view and a depiction of perspective that excludes unwanted visual "noise". Conceptualizing the visual relationships that will suggest an intended idea, however, can be challenging, because the resulting image should be easy to grasp in terms of both its literal and figurative connotations.

Malcolm X, director Spike Lee's biopic on the life of the eponymous African American civil rights activist, has a number of emblematic shots that reflect his personal and spiritual growth as well as the dynamics of his relationships with key figures who shaped his ideology and politics. Nowhere is this more evident than in a scene where Malcolm (Denzel Washington) gives a speech to a congregation of the Nation of Islam followers, exalting the wisdom of his mentor Elijah Muhammad (Al Freeman Jr.), the religious and political leader of the movement. At this point in the story, Malcolm's relationship with Elijah and the Nation of Islam

movement is at its strongest; he has proven to be a valuable asset, quickly ascending in the ranks and becoming famous for his articulate, charismatic, and impassioned speeches. The nature of Malcolm's connection with Elijah at this stage is reflected in a series of emblematic shots that feature a thoughtful juxtaposition of background and foreground elements to create symbolic meanings. In one of these shots, the camera is placed at a precise height while using a lens with a relatively normal focal length, allowing Malcolm to be seen standing directly in front of the mouth of a large portrait of Elijah in the background (left page, top frame); this powerful juxtaposition symbolically visualizes Malcolm's function as Elijah's mouthpiece, a role he is proud to fulfill but is not representative of his full contribution and potential as an activist for the movement. As the scene continues, the camera is placed at a lower angle and a lens with a longer focal length is used, compressing perspective in a way that makes Elijah's portrait appear to be much closer to Malcolm than previously (bottom). The telephoto's narrower field of view also eliminates ancillary visual information (the people on stage and even the context of the event), leaving the tension and focus strictly between the two men: Malcolm and Elijah. In this shot, Malcolm is positioned directly between the eyes of Elijah's looming portrait, making it seem as if Elijah is watching his actions closely. The composition effectively visualizes not just Elijah's tremendous influence on Malcolm, but also his larger than life persona, an attribute that would eventually create an ideological rift between them, leading to Malcolm's break from the Nation of Islam.

Batman Begins. *Christopher Nolan, Director; Wally Pfister, Cinematographer.* 2005.

MOVEMENT

At the extremes of the focal length range, wide-angle and telephoto lenses can alter the apparent speed of subjects in four fundamental ways. Wide-angle lenses can accelerate movement along the z-axis of the frame, because of the way they expand perspective, making subjects moving either toward or away from the camera look like they are covering a longer distance than they really are. Conversely, they can make movement along the x-axis of the frame appear slower than it really is, because they make the background behind a subject appear more distant, giving the impression that less distance is being covered. The perspective compression produced by telephoto lenses, on the other hand, makes subjects moving along the z-axis of the frame look as if they are advancing or receding at a slower speed because their size in the frame remains relatively unchanged, and therefore do not seem to be covering much distance. This effect is reversed with movement across the x-axis, which appears faster because the telephoto's narrow angle of view and perspective compression makes the background behind a moving subject cross the frame rapidly, giving the visual impression of speed. These speed distortions can be augmented or diminished when combined with camera movement or changes in the focal length within a shot (with zoom lenses), creating a multitude of dynamic variations that can support complex narrative meanings. A common practice when using these techniques, with or without camera movement, is to alternate the use of telephotos and wide-angles to accelerate and slow down the apparent speed of a subject, creating a greater visual impact and a more kinetic pace than what would be obtained if only one type of speed manipulation were used. In addition to altering movement in a seemingly physical, objective way, these techniques can also be used to externalize a character's psychological, subjective experience of how fast or slow their movement is, which may or may not match their actual speed.

Christopher Nolan's reboot of the Batman franchise, *Batman Begins*, marked the beginning of a gritty, more grounded approach to the superhero movie genre that incorporated story elements based on the imagined real-life consequences of a millionaire becoming a masked vigilante. Part of this realistic approach included Nolan's preference for physical effects over CGI, which resulted in most of the action scenes shot in camera in actual locations. These included an intense chase sequence that features several speed manipulations achieved through the use of wide-angle and telephoto lenses, conveying both objective changes in speed as well as a character's subjective experience of these changes. In one scene, as Batman rescues Rachel, his love interest, from the Scarecrow, a villain who poisoned her with a hallucinogenic toxin, he races to get an antidote while evading a throng of police cars chasing him; the shot on the left page, taken with a wide-angle lens, enhances the frenetic pace of the chase and the urgency of the scene, by accelerating the speed of Batman's "Tumbler" as it roars down an underpass. The expansion of perspective produced by this lens makes the features in the surrounding area (the overhead lights and beams, as well as the columns at the sides) recede into the distance much faster than they would if a normal or a telephoto lens had been used. The resulting effect is also complemented with a low-angle that not only makes the vehicle look more menacing, but also enhances the sense of speed by including much of the rapidly moving ground in the frame, providing one more visual cue that greatly accentuates its actual speed.

The narrow field of view and compressed perspective of telephoto lenses can greatly affect the apparent rate of movement along the frame's x-axis, making it appear significantly faster than it actually is. This technique can make subjects look like they are moving at great speed when the camera tracks along or pans with them because of how rapidly details in the background and/or foreground cross the frame (one of director Akira Kurosawa's signature techniques). The apparent acceleration is a function of the shorter distance visual elements have to cover between the sides of the frame because of the telephoto's narrower angle of view. For instance, a tree in the background of a sideways moving shot taken with a 50mm lens would cover a distance equivalent to a horizontal angle of view of 27°; if the same shot was taken with a 100mm lens, the tree would cover a distance equivalent to a horizontal angle of view of just 13.6°, and would therefore take half the time to cross the frame. The effect can therefore become more pronounced with longer focal lengths, especially when action is staged in spaces that have numerous visual elements between the subject and the camera, because they will appear to move faster than elements in the background due to the shorter horizontal distance they have to cover. However, longer focal lengths also make it much harder to keep moving subjects properly framed, especially in medium and tighter shots, and will also require longer distances between subject and camera because of the telephoto's magnification; even with wider framings, extensive preparation and rehearsals will be necessary to manage a shot of this kind.

Tom Tykwer's *Run Lola Run*, an unusual action thriller that examines three alternate outcomes for the same story, frequently uses telephoto lenses to show Lola (Franka Potente) running against the clock after she is given 20 minutes to save her boyfriend, Manni, from being killed by gangsters after misplacing a large sum of money. Much of the tension in this film comes from watching Lola run at a frenetic pace through the streets of Berlin, dodging all kinds of obstacles to make it in time; the kinetic energy of many of these scenes is largely due to the use of telephoto lenses at perpendicular angles to her movement, which make her look as if she is running much faster than she really is. A typical example occurs early during all three versions of her journey, as Lola runs by the side of a cemetery; the narrow field of view makes the wall behind her cross the frame so quickly it blurs (left page), providing a visual cue that exaggerates her actual speed. Although a longer focal length would have resulted in a more pronounced effect, the tighter framing would not have allowed enough of the cemetery in the background to be seen by the audience, preventing its symbolic association with death to serve as a reminder of the consequences should Lola fail to save Manni. The inclusion of trees and lamp posts between Lola and the camera (top left, right, and bottom right frames), however, make up for the relatively wide framing because they whiz across the frame acting as visual cues that reinforce the sense of speed. A longer focal length/tighter framing would also have made it impractical to keep Lola in the frame during the many extended running sequences included in this film.

THX 1138 George Lucas, Director; Albert Kihn, David Myers, Cinematographers, 1971

speed

A subject's apparent speed moving along the z-axis of the frame can be increased through the use of wide-angle lenses, due to the way they expand perspective; the shorter the focal length, the faster the perceived speed will appear to be. This speed manipulation can be further enhanced with the inclusion of relative size depth cues along the axis of movement, because they provide a spatial reference for how much ground is being covered by a subject. A location that includes numerous similar objects (like lamp posts, trees, or columns) can make the acceleration look more pronounced if they are positioned to pass as close to the lens as possible, maximizing the wide-angle's foreshortening effect when they enter or exit the frame. This technique can also be applied to instances where the camera remains stationary and a subject comes towards or speeds away from it: the closer it passes by the lens, the faster its speed will seem. Camera movement along the x or y axes that culminates as the moving subject is closest to the lens can also amplify the speed manipulation, as can moving the camera toward an incoming or away from an outgoing moving subject, effectively counterpointing its direction along the z-axis. Combining some or all of these manipulations to increase a subject's apparent speed with techniques designed to *slow down* perceived motion (one of which is examined in the next section) is often done, because alternating between them results in a more dramatic visual shift that makes the accelerated sections feel faster; it also prevents techniques that accelerate motion from becoming monotonous or even tiresome through

Director George Lucas uses this technique in *THX 1138*, a science-fiction film set in a dystopian, futuristic underground society where emotion-suppressive drugs are forced-fed, sexual intercourse is outlawed, and consumerism is mandatory. When the titular character (Robert Duvall) is found guilty of breaking these laws, he is deemed "incurable" and sentenced to indefinite detention, but manages to escape with the help of a human-looking sentient hologram. During the climax of the film, he steals a car and races down a labyrinth of deserted tunnels at breakneck speeds while chased by android policemen; the apparent speed of his car in this sequence is greatly enhanced by the use of an extreme wide-angle lens that expands perspective, strategically positioned close to walls (left page, top frame) and to the ground (bottom left) to make the physical depth cues in the location (lane markings and handrails) pass close to the camera. The short focal length also stylizes the overall look of the sequence by overtly showcasing its foreshortening effect on the tunnels and THX himself (bottom right), in a stark visual contrast with most of the scenes leading up to it, which were shot with telephoto lenses that compressed perspective and conveyed a claustrophobic, oppressive feel. This radical visual shift in the depiction of space, combined with the almost surreal acceleration of the car, communicate the concepts of "speed" and "escape" more as abstract notions than narrative plot points, and imbue this sequence with an experimental quality that mirrors Lucas' *Electronic Labyrinth THX 1138 4EB*, the short student film that inspired *THX 1138*.

Lawrence of Arabia. *David Lean, Director; Freddie Young, Cinematographer. 1962.*

Telephoto lenses can make subjects moving along the z-axis of the frame, either toward or away from the camera, appear to advance at a slower pace than they really are, because their size in the frame seems unchanged even if they are actually covering a considerable distance. This effect is a function of the long camera to subject distances needed to counteract the magnification of the telephoto lens, which in turn decreases the distance covered by a subject *relative to the camera's position*. For example, a subject in a medium shot advancing 5 feet toward a camera that is 10 feet away will have traversed half of the total distance, and therefore its size in the frame will change significantly as a result; but a subject in the same medium shot, advancing those same 5 feet, but taken with a telephoto lens positioned 100 feet away, will have covered only 1/20th of the total distance, and its size in the frame will seem unchanged, giving the impression that it hardly moved at all. The apparent lack of progress across space produced by this technique can be ideal for situations where the implication is that something or someone is having difficulty reaching a destination; the difficulty itself can take a physical form (as obstacles in the way, an overly long distance to be covered, or an unavoidable deadline, for instance), or be psychological in nature (reflecting a character's subjectivity in the way they perceive their own or someone else's lack of progress). The longer the focal length used, the more pronounced the effect will be, and with enough room to set up the camera far enough it is possible to make a subject look like they are not advancing at all, regardless of the actual distance they are covering.

One of the most famous examples of this technique happens in what has become a legendary scene from director David Lean's *Lawrence of Arabia*, shot with a custom 482mm telephoto lens with spherical optics created by Panavision[5] (dubbed the "David Lean Lens" ever since). When T.E. Lawrence (Peter O'Toole), a British army cartographer, is sent to learn Prince Feisal's plans for his revolt against the Turks, he embarks on a trek across a desert with a Bedouin guide. On the way, they stop to drink from a well when they spot a mirage far in the horizon: a black shape undulating under visible heat waves (left page, top left frame). After a few seconds, the figure takes the shape of a camel rider galloping toward them (top right), but still seemingly a long distance away (middle). Suddenly, the guide rushes to his camel and grabs a gun, but is shot dead by the rider, who somehow arrives at the well just a moment later. The extreme telephoto used on the distant rider, Sherif Ali (Omar Sharif), a tribesman protecting his well, showed such a compressed perspective that he hardly seemed to advance, effectively building up tension and adding suspense to the scene; this speed manipulation is enhanced by the cutting between looking shots of Lawrence (bottom left) and POV shots of the rider showing him at practically the same position until right after the shooting, where a long shot (bottom right) finally reveals their true relative distances. The distortion of the rider's apparent speed to conceal his actual location is also cleverly justified as a way to illustrate the deceptive nature of mirages and of the desert itself, presented in this film as a place of majestic beauty and unexpected dangers.

Punch-Drunk Love, Paul Thomas Anderson, Director; Robert Elswit, Cinematographer, 2002

desperation

Lens techniques rely on more than optical effects to communicate an idea; in some cases, specific features of a location can add an essential visual element to help create compelling, narratively expressive images. The physical qualities of a space (its color, architecture, scale) as well as its abstract qualities (its function, associated meanings, atmosphere) can complement or contradict the purpose of a lens technique, resulting in effective, compelling images, or ambiguous and even confounding shots. This concept is particularly important when using lens techniques that affect the apparent rate of movement within the frame, because these shots showcase a constant interaction between a subject and the space around them. Taking into account how a technique will interact with the concrete and/or abstract qualities of a space can be *the* determining factor when deciding which lens will achieve the most effective result. For instance, when trying to make a subject appear to move faster while in a space that has strong vertical elements, it may be more effective to use a telephoto lens while staging the action along the x-axis (as shown in the example from *Run Lola Run*), instead of using a wide-angle lens with movement staged along the z-axis of the frame (as seen in the example from *THX 1138*). In both instances motion will appear to be accelerated by correctly pairing direction of movement and focal length, but the technique that uses a telephoto lens will be more effective because the vertical features of the space will enhance the effect as the camera tracks the subject, making it appear to go faster than when using a wide-angle lens and motion along the z-axis.

Director Paul Thomas Anderson's romantic drama *Punch-Drunk Love* features a good example where lens choice is carefully coordinated with location attributes. Barry Egan (Adam Sandler) is a lonely, painfully shy, and socially inept man who falls in love with Lena, a woman who finds his awkwardness strangely appealing. After their first date, Barry bitterly regrets missing an obvious opportunity to kiss her, but when she calls to say she would have liked a kiss from him, he rushes back into her building but gets lost on the way to her apartment. His frustration and desperation, as he tries to figure out which way he should go, are visualized by a shot in which he runs at full speed down a long hallway. Taken with a telephoto lens, the shot compresses depth, making it appear as if he is hardly advancing (left page). The effect is further enhanced by the inclusion of several doorways in the composition that function as relative size depth cues, giving the audience a hint of the actual length of the hallway and the distance Barry must really be covering. The stylized framing of this shot also functions to briefly illustrate the inner conflict Barry is experiencing at this moment, as he struggles to overcome the crippling insecurities (symbolically represented by the "exit" signs) that stand in his way to win over Lena's affection. If the shot had been framed without the signs (by raising the camera into a higher angle, or by using a slightly tighter framing), this extra layer of meaning would have been lost. As shot, both the concrete and abstract attributes of the location perfectly complement the lens technique being used in a way that adds depth and sophistication to this scene and the narrative as a whole.

The coordination of camera movement with a lens' ability to manipulate the apparent speed of a subject will add a level of difficulty to the execution of a shot, but it can also open up exciting visual possibilities for creating expressive and meaningful images. Panning with a subject moving perpendicularly to the camera with a telephoto lens, for instance, will make its motion look accelerated across the x-axis of the frame, but as the subject keeps moving away from the camera, it would gradually appear to decelerate as its path gets closer to the z-axis: it would seem to change speed without actually doing so. Reversing this technique (by starting with movement along the z-axis and then along the x-axis) would have the opposite effect, making the subject appear to move at a slower pace at the beginning of a shot to then appear to pick up speed. The longer the focal length used, the more pronounced the shift between apparent speeds will be, but longer focal lengths will also require greater distances between camera and subject. As with all techniques that involve moving subjects, the difficulty is maintaining sharp focus throughout the shot, because of the constantly changing distance to the subject. A focus puller and careful choreography, as well as having preset focusing marks along the subject's path, are essential; using smaller apertures to increase the depth of field will also make keeping the subject in focus easier, provided enough light is available to avoid underexposure (or a higher ISO can be used without adding too much noise).

Notes on a Scandal, director Richard Eyre's psychological thriller about the toxic relationship that develops between Barbara, a high school history teacher nearing retirement, and Sheba (Cate Blanchett), a newly hired art teacher, expertly uses this technique to reflect a character's haste during a pivotal scene. When Barbara, who becomes pathologically attracted to Sheba, discovers she has been having a sexual relationship with one of her underage students, she seizes the opportunity to pressure her into spending time with her, by promising to keep Sheba's indiscretion secret as long she terminates her relationship with the boy. However, after she learns that Sheba has in fact continued her affair, she threatens to inform her husband unless she follows through with the breakup on the spot. Desperate to prevent this, Sheba rushes to the boy's home on a bicycle, shown in an extreme long shot taken with a telephoto lens that pans with her as she rides down the street. At the beginning of the shot (left page, top left and right frames) she hardly seems to advance because of the telephoto's perspective compression; however, as she gets closer and her path becomes more perpendicular to the camera (middle and bottom frames), she appears to pick up speed because the telephoto's narrow field of view shows the background shifting rapidly behind her. This apparent acceleration, produced by the way telephoto lenses affect motion differently along the z and x axes of the frame, effectively reflects the desperation this character feels at this moment, imbuing the scene with a palpable sense of urgency and haste. The frantic tone is compounded as Sheba rides closer to the camera, so close, in fact, that the audience is able to read the worried expression on her face.

Dolores Claiborne, Taylor Hackford, Director; Gabriel Beristain, Cinematographer, 1995

angst

Camera movement can be a powerful tool when combined with a lens' ability to manipulate how motion is perceived. The reduced field of view of telephoto lenses and its impact on movement along the x-axis, for instance, can produce an unusual effect when combined with a circular tracking camera move around a static subject, making it look as if the background is revolving quickly behind them. This effect can be enhanced by including highly visible landmarks or other location features behind the foreground subject, so that their motion as they shift across the frame is as noticeable as possible. The speed at which the background seems to move can be accelerated in three ways: by increasing the distance between it and the subject, by increasing the speed of the camera's circling move, and by using a telephoto with a very long focal length. Longer lenses, however, require placing the camera farther away from a subject to counteract the increased magnification of the image (especially when shooting medium and wider shots), which makes having locations with enough room for such setups indispensable. The unusual look produced by this technique is ideal to visualize a character's psychological breakdown or extreme inner turmoil during particularly stressful or emotionally intense situations, making it seem as if the world is spinning out of control around them.

Director Taylor Hackford's psychological thriller *Dolores Claiborne*, based on the novel of the same name by Stephen King, has an elegant use of this technique, in a scene where a character makes a life-changing discovery about her childhood. The story follows Selena (Jennifer Jason Leigh), a depressed and alcoholic journalist, as she returns to her Maine hometown to defend her mother Dolores after she is accused of murdering a wealthy woman she worked for as a maid. Their already estranged relationship reaches a breaking point when Dolores reveals that she killed Selena's father after discovering he was sexually abusing her. Angered and troubled by her mother's revelation, she decides to leave her to fend for herself; however, while on a ferry out of town, the sight of a bench triggers a repressed memory of her father molesting her to resurface. This moment is shown in a flashback that reflects the increasingly emotional and physical pain she feels as she gradually realizes her mother was not lying about her father's sexual abuse. Seeing herself as a child (Ellen Muth) sitting next to her father (David Strathairn), she witnesses his sexual assault (left page, top left frame). At this moment, the island in the background gradually begins to move from right to left, slowly picking up speed as her anguish intensifies (top right, middle, and bottom left). Right before she is snapped out of it by a ferry attendant (bottom right), the background is moving so rapidly Selena looks as if she were on an out of control merry-go-round, visualizing her inner turmoil as she vividly recalls the horrific truth. In reality, this shot was achieved by having the ferry gently turn about at the beginning of the scene, but the long telephoto lens magnified the distant background to such a degree that even this modest camera move, combined with an extremely narrow field of view, made it appear to shift rapidly behind her, resulting in an extremely effective depiction of her mental distress.

Bad Boys II, Michael Bay, Director; Amir Mokri, Cinematographer, 2003

resolve

Creating the illusion that the background of a shot shifts rapidly behind a static character in the foreground can visualize their intense emotional and/or psychological reaction to a meaningful discovery. This telephoto/dynamic camera technique (sometimes referred to as a "parallax shot") can also be combined with other visual stylizations to suggest more nuanced narrative situations and specific character traits. Choices in lighting, composition, exposure, art direction, frame rate, and music, among others, can contribute their own associated meanings to the overall effect of the technique, and directly influence how it will be interpreted by an audience. However, combining multiple techniques designed to overtly stylize a shot can be distracting if overused, so it should be reserved for a particularly meaningful moment of a story.

Michael Bay's *Bad Boys II*, the action comedy follow-up to his directorial debut, *Bad Boys*, features a scene that combines several techniques designed to stylize the look of a pivotal moment to underline its narrative significance, including the use of a telephoto lens with a dolly arc move to make the background appear to move at a high rate of speed around static subjects in the foreground. Although known for sometimes using over-the-top visuals indiscriminately, Bay deftly incorporates form and content in this scene, effectively communicating to the audience that a "point of no return" has been reached by Miami Police Department detectives Mike Lowrey (Will Smith) and Marcus Burnett (Martin Lawrence). The film follows their investigation of Johnny Tapia, a powerful and ruthless Cuban drug lord; after they manage to confiscate 100 million dollars from him, they receive a call where he demands his money back in exchange for Syd, Marcus' sister, whom he has abducted. The shot that follows showcases Mike and Marcus' reaction to Tapia's demands in a way that leaves no doubt that a critical line has been crossed. As the camera tracks around a rising Marcus in slow motion, a lens flare flashes behind him, briefly showing him in a classic "hero shot" (a technique examined on page 137). The long telephoto lens used for the tracking move makes the highway overpasses in the background shift rapidly behind him in an unnatural, almost surrealistic way (thanks to the camera move's high rate of speed, necessary because of the slow motion), while the narrow field of view crops them in a way that makes them appear like abstract diagonal shapes that further stylize the look of the shot (top right, middle, and bottom). Although this technique is commonly used to convey a character's inner turmoil (as seen in the example from *Dolores Claiborne* in the previous section) or psychological vulnerability, in this instance the shot's composition and the context of the scene give it a wholly different meaning: the extreme low-angle suggests Marcus and Mike feel emboldened instead of vulnerable, determined to take on impossible odds to rescue Marcus' sister from the drug lord. The combination of camera movement, slow motion, a lens flare, and a highly compressed perspective elevate what could have been a bland expository scene into a visually striking, kinetic, and memorable moment that fittingly supports the rather colorful statement Marcus makes about the surprising turn of events.

Election. *Alexander Payne, Director; James Glennon, Cinematographer. 1999.*

FOCUS

The ability to guide the audience's attention by keeping a specific area of the frame in sharp focus while everything else is more or less blurry is a powerful technique for creating visual emphasis and narrative meaning. For most of the history of motion pictures, however, the ability to use selective focus was primarily available only to filmmakers who shot on 35mm film, since smaller formats and the shorter lenses they use make it difficult to produce images with shallow depth of field. The introduction of video-capable DSLRs effectively ended this disparity, giving independent and low-budget filmmakers full access to this essential tool of cinematography (for more on this topic, check *The Lens Revolution* chapter). The expressive potential of selective focus, however, is often underutilized and/or misunderstood by beginners, who tend to concentrate their attention mostly on the focused areas of the frame, instead of considering what the interplay of focused (sharp) and out of focus (soft) visual elements in an image can convey as a whole. When used thoughtfully, out of focus areas in a frame can complement, contextualize, and inform what is in focus, suggesting relationships between visual elements that can communicate specific meanings to an audience, which can also be further developed when implemented dynamically over the duration of a shot by shifting focus (by rack and/or follow focusing). It is helpful to stop thinking of subjects in a shot as being simply "out of focus", and instead consider that you have a range of levels of detail at your disposal to produce meaning. When using selective focus in a shot, ask yourself: do I want areas of the frame to be only slightly soft so that much visual detail remains visible, or perhaps blurry enough so that the general shape of things can be seen but most details cannot, or maybe it's best to make things so out of focus

they become unrecognizable abstract shapes? The narrative possibilities of approaching selective focus in this way are vast, but require having complete control over the depth of field variables: the lens aperture, the intensity of the lights, the camera to subject distance, and the focal length of the lens.

Alexander Payne's *Election*, a dark comedy about the personal battle that ensues between Tracy Flick (Reese Witherspoon), an obnoxious, overachieving student dead set on winning her high school election, and her civics professor Jim McAllister, a man having a mid-life crisis who does not want her to win, includes a great example of using selective focus to shift narrative emphasis in a single shot. On election day, Tracy offers Jim a cupcake with her campaign slogan written in icing; this moment is shown in a medium close-up that racks focus from her face in the background (top frame) to the cupcake she is holding in the foreground (bottom), letting the audience read its message. Even though her face is out of focus at this point in the shot, we can still make out her perky smile, due to the aperture, camera to subject distance, and focal length combination used to get this precise level of blurriness. If the shot had used a depth of field that kept both foreground and background in focus simultaneously, the audience's attention would have been divided between them, and the visual punchline provided by the rack focus would not have been possible. Alternatively, if a shallower depth of field had been used, her face would have been too blurry to let the audience notice her irritating smile throughout the shot. Instead, the precise level of blurriness allowed the rack focus to dynamically shift the narrative emphasis within the frame for both comedic effect and to underline Tracy's bumptious, overbearing attitude.

Most audiences are unaware of the constant cutting that happens when they watch a film; this is not surprising, since most editing techniques are designed to be invisible, so that story, and not the filmmaking process, takes center stage. There are instances, however, when filmmakers purposely avoid editing and choose instead to let a moment play out in real time, keeping the spatial and temporal unity of a scene intact. This may be done for a variety of reasons: to preserve the emotional intensity and original pacing of an actor's performance, or to signal that a moment has a special significance, or to build up tension and/or suspense. In the absence of editing to direct the audience's attention to relevant details in a scene, one alternative is to use rack focusing, a technique where the focusing plane is shifted between two or more subjects along the z-axis of the frame during a take. Generally, one subject is placed near the camera in the foreground and one in the middle ground or background of the shot, with a depth of field shallow enough to keep only one of them in sharp focus. The level of blurriness can play a significant role in how the effect is perceived by an audience, which can be especially important in scenes that include some type of character interaction. For instance, if the rack focus is done with a depth of field so shallow it prevents the audience from registering the facial features of the character out of focus, their attention will be mostly drawn to the character in sharp focus; however, if the level of blurriness allows enough visual detail for the demeanor of the character out of focus to be noticed, then their attention will be divided between them, adding a context that can influence how their exchange is understood. The speed at which the plane of focus is shifted can also influence tone and mood; if the racking is swift, it can come across as the equivalent of a quick cut, speeding up the pace of a scene. If, however, the racking is performed slowly, it can generate suspense and/or tension. This effect can be made more overt or subtle by controlling the depth of field to make the shift between focusing planes more or less dramatic.

A classic example of a rack focus, used to imply that an exchange of glances carries a special significance, occurs near the end of director Richard Ayoade's brilliant coming-of-age comedy *Submarine*, the story of Oliver (Craig Roberts), a nerdy, socially awkward teenager who becomes infatuated with Jordana (Yasmin Paige), a feisty, free-spirited girl who throws his life into turmoil. After a whirlwind romance, Oliver briefly becomes Jordana's boyfriend until she breaks up with him over a slight; in the last scene of the film, he tries to convince her to take him back, but she refuses, so he simply stands silently next to her (left page, top frame). After he notices she is staring at him, the focus racks to her, revealing a hint of a smile (bottom left). Oliver then stares ahead as the focus racks back to him, showing him holding back a smile of his own (bottom right). Using a rack focus (instead of a conventional shot/reverse shot) to guide our attention through their unspoken exchange not only underlines the significance of this moment and reveals they still have feelings for each other, but also creates an emotional rhythm that would be lost if both of them had been shown in sharp focus simultaneously.

context

Selective focus gives a filmmaker the ability to direct an audience's attention to specific areas of a frame, which ultimately influences how they understand the shot's meaning. The degree of blurriness in out of focus areas, however, should be adjusted according to how much visual detail is needed to understand the narrative point of the shot, because different levels of visual information can communicate different degrees of tension, emotional engagement, and many other narrative contexts/subtexts. For this reason, selective focus should not be seen as a binary concept (things are either sharp or blurry), but as a spectrum with many different gradations, each capable of producing distinct meanings.

Director Jessica Hausner's *Lourdes*, the story of Christine (Sylvie Testud), a lonely, wheelchair-bound young woman with multiple sclerosis who visits the eponymous pilgrim's destination, features a brilliant use of selective focus in a shot that illustrates how precise control over the off-focus level can visually and subtly enhance the drama and generate tension. In this poignant scene, Christine listens as Maria (Léa Seydoux), a volunteer in charge of assisting her, reveals that her search for meaning prompted her to come to Lourdes to help others. This is shown in a medium long shot with a semi-shallow depth of field that keeps the action in the foreground in focus, but does not show enough sharp detail in the background to distract from the moment where Christine listens to Maria's confession (left page). In the slightly soft background, male volunteers can be seen whispering to each other while glancing at Maria, in a manner that suggests they are talking about her. Showing the volunteers in the background with a slightly soft focus allows the audience to concentrate their attention on the women's dialogue, body language, and facial expressions, but to a lesser degree also showcases the men's behavior; this allows their inclusion in the shot to subtly and unobtrusively visualize Christine and Maria's shared preoccupation with men and the irony behind their respective emotional woes. Just as Maria expresses her desire for a more meaningful life, the demeanor of the volunteers appears to exemplify the type of social interaction she is trying to avoid by coming to Lourdes; for Christine, however, they represent the kind of male attention she desperately wishes she could elicit, especially from one particular volunteer whom she finds attractive. This thoughtful manipulation of depth of field to precisely control the level of visual detail in the background adds another dimension to their conversation, revealing a context that is not directly alluded to but that nevertheless connects these characters. It also subtly illustrates some of the larger themes of *Lourdes'* story: the dichotomy between the spiritual and the physical, between faith and desire, and between the sacred and the profane. If this scene had been shot with a deep depth of field, keeping both the background and the foreground in sharp focus (and allowing the men to potentially distract audiences from the nuances of Maria and Christine's conversation), or a much shallower depth of field that completely blurred the background (preventing the men's body language from being seen), it would not have been possible to incorporate this level of contextual complexity, narrative sophistication, and audience engagement

significance

The minimum focusing distance of most lenses prevents placing subjects closer than a couple of feet from the camera and still remain in focus. However, there are specialized lenses, called macros, that make it possible to keep a subject in focus at much closer distances, in some cases even right next to the lens (discussed on page 49). The extremely short minimum focusing distance of macros allows them to greatly magnify tiny details that would otherwise be hard or impossible to see with the naked eye. However, using a macro lens on a subject or a detail of a subject will not only magnify it visually, but will also magnify its implied importance in a story, as suggested by Hitchcock's Rule ("the size of an object on screen should be proportional to its significance at that moment"[2]). It is therefore important to have a narratively compelling reason to use a macro lens on a subject, whether the justification is immediately obvious or revealed at a later time in the story, to avoid letting the extreme magnification come across as narratively misleading, stylistically gratuitous, and ultimately unnecessary.

A particularly effective example of the use of a macro lens can be seen in director Steven Spielberg's historical drama *Schindler's List*, the story of how Oskar Schindler (Liam Neeson), a German businessman, managed to save more than a thousand Jewish refugees from certain death during the Holocaust by employing them in one of his factories. Originally only interested in war profiteering, Schindler has a change of heart when he witnesses the extent of the mass executions committed by Nazi soldiers while relocating Jewish refugees from a ghetto into a concentration camp.

When the Schutzstaffel (SS) decides to transport more prisoners westward into the death camp at Auschwitz, Schindler bribes Nazi officials so that he can keep 1200 of them to work for him, effectively saving their lives. At the climax of the film, Schindler and Itzhak Stern (Ben Kingsley), a well-connected Jewish official he recruited, put together a list of names of those who will be saved, in a sequence that underscores the gravity and urgency of the situation (left page, top left frame). As Stern types a name (top right), extreme close-ups of the typewriter striking last names are shown; this scene is intercut with Schindler bribing SS commandant Goeth, the inhuman Nazi officer who runs the concentration camp where the refugees are kept, while also trying to convince another profiteer to keep his own Jewish workers from being moved to Auschwitz. When we return to the making of the list, even tighter shots of individual letters being typed, taken with a macro lens, have replaced the extreme close-ups shown previously (bottom), magnifying details to such degree that the texture of the paper itself can be seen. The individual names are not shown at this stage; the extreme closeness emphasizes instead the process of creating the list itself, the vital significance of every single letter being added. Upon completing his arduous task, Stern declares: "The list is an absolute good...the list...is life...," underscoring the symbolic connection between the list he just typed and the lives it will save. It is difficult to imagine that this sequence would have the same emotional impact without the use of macro shots magnifying every detail of the making of the list, effectively visualizing its crucial, life-affirming significance.

shock

Focus pulling, the adjustment of a lens' focusing ring during the taking of a shot, can provide an effective way to underscore a character's reaction at seeing something especially meaningful. The technique involves a variation of the traditional looking shot/POV/reaction shot editing pattern, where the POV starts blurry but is then progressively brought into sharp focus (instead of being in focus from the beginning), before cutting back to the character's reaction shot. The focus pull is done slowly, gradually revealing what the character is looking at, adding tension and suspense to the moment, but also reflecting the mental process of slowly coming to a full realization of what they are seeing (rather than the instantaneous identification implied by a traditional POV shot). Slow motion and an empathetic music cue are often used in conjunction with this technique, because without them the audience could mistake the focus pull as visualizing the subjectivity of a character with vision problems, instead of reflecting their psychological or emotional state at that moment. Because of the highly unusual stylization produced by this technique, it should be reserved to showcase only extreme reactions to something or someone of significant relevance to the story.

Quentin Tarantino's revisionist take on the western genre, *Django Unchained*, features an effective focus pull POV shot that conveys a character's shock and disbelief in a particularly tense scene. Set in the South two years before the start of the American Civil War, *Django* tells the story of the eponymous character (Jamie Foxx), a slave who is recruited by Dr. King Schultz (Christoph Waltz), a bounty hunter who needs his help identifying a trio of fugitives. Django agrees to help Schultz if he in turn helps him locate his wife, who they eventually discover is in Candieland, a plantation owned by a sadistic slaver, prompting them to hatch a plan to rescue her. Their arrival at Candieland is witnessed by Stephen (Samuel L. Jackson), the "head house slave" in charge of the plantation who acts submissive in public but maintains an extremely informal, at times dominant relationship with Calvin behind closed doors. As Stephen catches sight of Django entering Candieland dressed like a free man, armed, and riding a horse next to a white man (unthinkable at the time), his look goes from sheer shock (left page, top left frame) to scorn and contempt (bottom right); in his eyes, Django's apparent equality among whites (a point underlined by the use of a balanced shot composition) is an affront to the slave system under which he has thrived. These emotions are eloquently expressed not only in Stephen's looking and reaction shots, but also by the gradual focus pull used in the slow motion POV shot of Django and Schultz entering the estate, which gradually goes from blurry to tack sharp (top right, middle left and right, and bottom left), as a momentous march plays in the soundtrack. The focus pull in this shot suggests that the sight of a free, proud black man riding alongside whites is too much for Stephen to take in all at once, and he needs time to process the implications of what he is seeing. The extreme visual stylization of this moment not only underlines Stephen's harsh reaction to seeing Django, but also serves to give him one of the most memorable character introductions of this film.

The Machinist. *Brad Anderson, Director; Xavi Giménez, Cinematographer. 2004.*

denial

A shallow depth of field can be a useful tool to reveal or conceal characters, by having them enter or exit a predetermined area of sharp focus (usually in the foreground of a shot). In a reveal, this technique can make a dramatic visual statement about the importance of a character in a story, by protracting the time it takes an audience to see them in full detail, adding suspense and tension to their appearance (which explains why this kind of reveal is often used in character introductions). In a conceal, the technique can convey a wholly different meaning: as a character is shown first in sharp focus in the foreground and then gradually out of focus as they move away, the implication can be that their involvement with the story is coming to an end, often signaling that they will not be seen again. The shallow depth of field is usually achieved by setting the focus to a short camera to subject distance, at times complemented with a wide aperture to produce a higher level of blurriness in the middle ground and background of the shot. Although not strictly necessary, sometimes slow motion and/or other techniques that further stylize the look of the shot are added to enhance the effect and to underline the uniqueness of the moment (as seen in the example from *Django Unchained* in the previous section).

The Machinist, director Brad Anderson's psychological thriller about Trevor Reznick (Christian Bale), a factory worker who suffers from extreme insomnia and becomes emaciated because of it, includes a brilliant use of shallow depth of field in a visual conceal that ironically serves to *reveal* the cause of his condition. As Trevor's health worsens, he gets harassed by a coworker, Ivan, who stalks him every-

where he goes. Trevor finds solace from this ordeal when he befriends a waitress, Maria, and her son, Nicholas. Upon discovering that Ivan threatens their safety too, he murders him. However, after Ivan's body strangely disappears, Trevor finally realizes that Nicholas, Maria, and Ivan were actually figments of his imagination, and that he was, in fact, responsible for the death of a child in a hit and run accident a year earlier. His extreme insomnia was caused by the deep remorse he suppressed from his conscious mind. Ivan was nothing more than the embodiment of Trevor's growing sense of guilt, psychologically torturing him as his health deteriorated. This key revelation is shown in a flashback that includes a shot that visualizes Trevor's impulse to block his memory of the accident. After a close-up of his stunned face looking healthy (left page, top left frame) and a POV shot of a woman identical to Maria kneeling over the child he hit with his car (top right), he is seen speeding away in a progressively canted slow motion shot that renders him gradually out of focus as he recedes into the distance (middle left, middle right, and bottom). The combination of the canted angle, the slow motion, and the prolonged blurriness of this shot suggests that something of an unusual nature is happening; within the context of the story, as Trevor goes out of focus the implication is that the person he is at this critical moment, both physically and psychologically, will cease to exist. As he drives away to avoid taking responsibility for the child's death, he also symbolically leaves behind his conscious memory of it, embracing instead a denial that leads him to a severe mental and physical breakdown.

The Innocents, Jack Clayton, Director; Freddie Francis, Cinematographer, 1961

foreboding

Selective focus uses a shallow depth of field to render a chosen area of the frame in sharp focus while the rest of the image is blurred; however, there are times when a filmmaker may want everything in the frame to be seen clearly. In these cases, "deep focus", a technique refined by directors such as Jean Renoir and Orson Welles and embraced by contemporary filmmakers like Terrence Malick and Alejandro G. Iñárritu, offers not just unique visual storytelling possibilities, but also a special kind of audience engagement because of its lack of selective focus. In deep focus cinematography, the foreground, middleground, and background planes are in sharp focus simultaneously, making it possible to showcase multiple subjects and their surrounding area; however, since everything is shown with the same level of sharpness, the audience has to choose precisely what is narratively important in the frame and therefore deserving of their attention. This technique is often paired with carefully choreographed blocking and camera movement to highlight key visual elements, and generally features long takes to provide audiences with enough time to scan the frame. Since everything is in sharp focus, it is especially important to pay attention to details of the mise en scène that would normally be concealed in areas of blurriness; because of this, deep focus shots often require extra work from almost every department in a film crew, and have become somewhat of a "lost art" in contemporary filmmaking despite their ability to make a unique visual statement. Creating deep focus requires a small aperture (and enough light to compensate, or a higher ISO) and setting a lens to the hyperfocal distance, which results in

making everything within half of that distance and infinity sharp. Although hyperfocal distance produces the deepest depth of field possible for a given aperture, it has a limit to how close a subject can be to the camera while still in focus; this distance, however, can be decreased by using wide-angle lenses. If subjects need to be even closer, split-field diopters (examined in the next section) offer an alternative that produces a similar look.

Jack Clayton's superb psychological horror film, *The Innocents*, deftly uses deep focus cinematography to set an ominous atmosphere as it tells the story of a governess who suspects the children under her care are possessed by ghosts. After her employer leaves on a long trip, Miss Giddens (Deborah Kerr) notices a strange couple randomly appear throughout the estate. When she learns they are in fact the previous governess, who killed herself, and her lover, who died under mysterious circumstances, she suspects their ghosts are behind the uncanny behavior of the children, Miles and Flora (Martin Stephens, Pamela Franklin), who at times act and speak as if they were adults. The setting, an isolated gothic mansion, is imbued with an eerie ambience with the help of low-key lighting, but deep focus cinematography also adds a palpable sense of dread and tension by showcasing every dark corner, crevice, and piece of furniture as if they were characters in and of themselves. This has the effect of giving every scene with Miss Giddens and the children (left page), even those where nothing sinister actually happens, a foreboding quality that gives credence to her belief that their behavior is connected to the apparitions.

Mission: Impossible. *Brian De Palma, Director; Stephen H. Burum, Cinematographer. 1996 (top).*
The Departed. *Martin Scorsese, Director; Michael Ballhaus, Cinematographer. 2006 (bottom).*

tension

Although split-field diopters (a partial lens attachment that functions just like bifocal glasses) are not used as often as they were during the 1970s, they are making something of a comeback, and their use can be seen in films by some of the most famous directors working today. These lens attachments produce images that effectively have two distinct focusing planes, allowing subjects both near and far to be in sharp focus simultaneously, in a way that would not be possible with conventional lenses because of depth of field limitations. This look is reminiscent of deep focus cinematography, with the difference that in deep focus shots everything is sharp, but in split-field diopter shots there is an area of blurriness where the diopter ends. This "seam" is sometimes purposely concealed by placing it over a featureless area in the location or along a strong vertical edge within the shot. Additionally, while setting a lens to a hyperfocal distance (as seen in the example in the previous section) can produce a similar look, it does not allow having a subject in sharp focus as close to the camera to produce the same striking visual effect. The unique focusing characteristics of split-field diopters are often used to visualize meaningful emotional or psychological connections between characters, particularly during tense or uneasy situations.

Director Brian De Palma's *Mission: Impossible* has a classic example of a split-field diopter shot, in a scene where Ethan Hunt (Tom Cruise), a daredevil spy unjustly accused of betraying his agency, attempts to steal a document to prove his innocence from a secured vault at the CIA's headquarters. As he is lowered from a vent to avoid detection, an agent (Rolf Saxon) suddenly enters, unaware of Ethan's presence; at this point a low-angle shot that uses a split-field diopter (left page, top frame) shows they are seemingly only a few feet apart, and that Ethan is dangerously close to being discovered. The diopter helps reinforce the dramatic tension of this moment by showing both characters in sharp focus simultaneously; if the shot had been taken without it, Ethan would have looked significantly less vulnerable since either him or the agent would have been out of focus and therefore partially concealed from view. Unorthodox framing choices complement the awkwardness of this moment, from the way the agent's head sticks out from one corner of the frame at a canted angle, to the extreme low-angle that shows Ethan as if he were standing rather than hanging from the ceiling.

Martin Scorsese's *The Departed*, a retelling of Andrew Lau and Alan Mak's superb crime thriller *Infernal Affairs*, also features a split-field diopter in a key scene that visualizes the unspoken tension that exists between Colin Sullivan (Matt Damon), a mole for the Irish mob who infiltrated the Massachusetts State Police, and Madolyn Madden (Vera Farmiga), a police psychiatrist romantically involved with him. Madolyn suspects Colin is hiding something when he gets a phone call and acts guarded, during a scene where both are shown in sharp focus thanks to a split-field diopter (bottom). The unusual focusing effect reflects both the importance of the phone call (by keeping Colin sharp in a close-up that takes up half of the frame in the foreground), and Madolyn's deepening suspicions despite his efforts to conceal his dealings.

concentration

When the aim is to bring an audience into the personal space of a character, few shots can do a better job than the close-up, which allows a filmmaker to showcase facial nuances of an actor's performance, letting viewers connect with them, and the story, on an emotional level. Depth of field can enhance the sense of intimacy a close-up communicates, because of the way it can mimic human vision in situations when we are so close to an object that our eyes can only focus on a detail instead of a whole figure. A shallow depth of field can suggest this effect by keeping only a portion of an actor's face sharp, making it seem as though we are so close that we cannot see the entire face in focus (even if the shot is taken with a telephoto lens from a considerable distance). This technique requires careful consideration regarding which areas of a character's face should be in focus and which should be slightly soft or downright blurry, because of the way any facial feature shown in focus will be interpreted as being especially meaningful and important to understanding the context of the shot and the scene. The decision of what should be showcased depends on what needs to be communicated to an audience; although keeping the eyes of a character in sharp focus might seem the obvious choice in many situations, other features might work just as well if they are more relevant to the moment and its intended meaning. For instance, maintaining sharp focus on an ear can imply that a character is listening intently to something or waiting for some aural signal, while keeping a drop of sweat running down a cheek in focus can imply they are under intense pressure or experiencing extreme anxiety.

Director Bennett Miller's film *Capote*, based on the events surrounding the grisly murders of a Kansas family that inspired Truman Capote's non-fiction novel *In Cold Blood*, features a scene that uses a close-up with a shallow depth of field that brilliantly captures the essence of a pivotal moment of the story. After spending months charming and even bribing members of the community and local police to gain inside information about the case and access to the killers to conduct interviews, Truman (Philip Seymour Hoffman) decides to write a book instead of an article about the murders, inventing a new literary genre in the process: the non-fiction novel. This key moment of inspiration is dramatized in a scene that opens with a tight close-up of his face (left page, top frame) with a shallow depth of field that only allows his eyes and part of his nose to be in sharp focus, underlining the intensity of his concentration as he starts typing what would eventually become *In Cold Blood*. The feeling of physical closeness and intimacy elicited by the use of selective focus in this case directs the audience's attention to the professional resolve in his gaze, revealing a very different persona than the one they have seen up to this point. This is not Truman the dissipated raconteur and socialite; this is Truman the innovative and disciplined writer, completely absorbed by the story he is writing. The following shot (bottom), provides a sharp contrast between the subjectivity visualized by the close-up, showing him from a more physically distant, objective perspective that suggests, through a high-angle, the hard, solitary, and unglamorous work needed to bring his ideas to the page.

Although character close-ups can be taken with a wide range of focal lengths, the resulting images will have distinct looks and *feel* different from one another, even if everything else about them (composition, lighting style, depth of field) is similar. This is a function of the different types of distortion that occur to a face because of the various distances needed to frame a close-up with a given focal length. For instance, when shooting with a wide-angle lens, the short camera to subject distance makes barrel distortion more evident, while the longer distances needed with telephoto lenses result in the flattening of facial features (a concept that is discussed on page 42). Audiences may not be aware of the technical reasons behind these looks, but can tell that some shots feel distant while others feel closer and more intimate. Experienced filmmakers are aware of this effect, and often pick a lens based on the level of physical closeness and intimacy they want an audience to feel at a given moment. A wide-angle lens may be used for a character's close-up when the aim is to make us feel as if we are within their personal space (even uncomfortably so), potentially eliciting a strong emotional connection. Likewise, a telephoto lens may be used instead if the aim is to make us feel distant and emotionally detached from a character, maybe even to add a voyeuristic element to our engagement.

Alejandro G. Iñárritu's historical survival drama, *The Revenant*, includes a series of shots where the implied physical proximity of the audience to a character is manipulated to signal that a life-changing event is taking place. Set in the early years of the 19th century in territories that would become the Dakotas, the story follows frontiersman Hugh Glass' (Leonardo DiCaprio) harrowing quest for survival after he is left for dead following a bear attack. Cinematographer Emmanuel Lubezki creates a visceral visual experience with wide-angle lenses and a deep depth of field that consistently showcases the natural beauty of the wilderness setting, which also necessitated very short distances from subjects when shooting close-ups. However, there were times when the filmmakers wanted to bring the audience even closer to Glass' face than the 7" (the minimum focusing distance) the 14mm lens they were using would allow. Lubezki solved this problem by adding two master diopter attachments (in essence magnifying glasses) that allowed the camera to be only 4" away, close enough for DiCaprio's breath to momentarily fog the lens, while also exacerbating the lens' barrel distortion and adding noticeable chromatic aberrations to the edges of the frame.[7] The resulting images have a surreal, dreamlike quality that was appropriately reserved for three key moments when Glass' life is irrevocably changed, in a sense undergoing a symbolic rebirth: when he learns the fate of his son (left page, bottom left), after he survives a freezing night inside a horse's carcass (bottom right), and during the dramatic end of his journey (top). The extreme stylization of these shots, produced by the unusually close camera to subject distance made possible by the use of diopters, serves to visualize Glass' complex emotional and psychological reaction to these momentous events, allowing the audience to connect with his plight in a unique way that would not have been possible using conventional lenses.

Prisoners, Denis Villeneuve, Director; Roger Deakins, Cinematographer, 2013

impairment

Using selective focus to visualize a character's subjectivity is among the oldest lens techniques in the history of cinema; early examples can be seen in German Expressionist films from the 1920s. It continues to be used to this day because it is an extremely effective way to let an audience experience a character's physical, emotional, or psychological state, especially in unusual or particularly tense situations. One variation of this technique involves using it in combination with a looking/POV/reaction shot sequence – one of cinema's most effective methods for eliciting audience identification with a character. For instance, to show someone is experiencing a visual impairment, we would start with a shot of a character looking at something, followed by a POV shot that visualizes their impairment (by showing an out of focus or otherwise degraded image), and then return to the character to show their reaction. The degree of image deterioration in these types of POV shots should reflect the severity of the visual disability being experienced by the character, and can also incorporate other visual tropes (like canted angles and unbalanced compositions) to represent conditions caused by drugs, physical injuries, or extreme psychological states. The POV shots in this technique are almost always subjective shots that show things as if seen through the eyes of a character, prompting the audience to identify with their plight. However, subjective shots can quickly feel gimmicky if used too often or for too long, so it is important to restrict their use to particularly meaningful moments.

A brilliant use of selective focus to convey a character's physical impairment can be found in an especially tense scene from Denis Villeneuve's *Prisoners*, a thriller that examines the moral dilemmas a suburban couple face after they kidnap and torture a creepy loner they believe abducted their 6-year-old daughter. After Loki (Jake Gyllenhaal), a detective determined to solve the case, chances upon the suspect's aunt in the process of poisoning the kidnapped girl, he manages to kill the woman during a shootout but ends up bleeding from a head wound. Forced to get the girl medical attention as quickly as possible he drives her to a hospital, in a nerve-racking scene where he speeds dangerously through traffic during a heavy snowstorm at night. As he rushes through stoplights and narrowly avoids hitting other cars, his already perilous situation worsens when blood from his wound covers his right eye (left page, top left frame), severely diminishing his vision. This physical impairment is reflected with a subjective shot (top right) in which the entire field of view is out of focus, preventing him from seeing how close the cars in front of him really are. When Loki tries to clear his vision (bottom left) his situation worsens, as only the car's windshield is in focus (bottom right), while the traffic ahead is reduced to a handful of bokeh highlights that make judging relative distances impossible. This simple focusing technique works extremely well in this scene, because it not only allows the audience to experience Loki's physical impairment first hand, but also because of the use of two different POV shots that show different levels of blurriness, indicating that his situation is not only extremely vulnerable but worsening with every second that passes, adding an extra level of strain to an already unbearably tense scene.

Sideways, Alexander Payne, Director; Phedon Papamichael, Cinematographer, 2004

turmoil

As with any other technical element in cinema, there are uses for a lens that ordinarily might be considered unconventional, unexpected, or even a technical blunder, but in an appropriate context can be precisely expressive. For example, when a character repeatedly enters or leaves a narrow area of sharp focus; this is a common problem when shooting shallow depth of field close-ups with an over-active actor who inadvertently leans too far forward or back, causing their focus to go soft. However, subverting the convention to consistently maintain facial features under sharp focus, even during character movement, can be used as an effective way to visualize a character's distorted subjectivity. Allowing a character to move in and out of a fixed range of focus can convey an altered perception due to a physical impairment, or an extreme emotional reaction, such as panic or anxiety. This technique is often paired with other stylizations to amplify its visual impact, like unorthodox framing and unconventional editing techniques, which also ensure the momentary blurriness is understood as an intentional aesthetic choice expressing a precise emotional and narrative meaning, and not an instance of technical sloppiness.

Sideways, Alexander Payne's comedy/drama about a wine-tasting road trip taken by lifelong friends Miles (Paul Giamatti), a divorced, humorless wine aficionado, and Jack, an actor past his prime looking for a fling before his wedding, features an interesting use of this technique that visualizes both a physical impairment and an altered emotional state. While on a double date with a local waitress and her friend, Miles gets drunk and decides to call his ex-wife in a

last ditch attempt to reconcile with her before she remarries, but his conversation ends abruptly after she realizes he is intoxicated (left page, top left frame). During this call, he is shown in a series of extreme close-ups with a shallow depth of field (due to the close proximity of the lens to Miles' face) that makes him go in and out of focus with every slight movement of his body. The seemingly random blurriness in these shots is complemented with the use of an unsteady, haphazard handheld camera and shot compositions that lack clear focal points (top right, middle, and bottom left), adding to the jarring, disjointed quality of this moment. This technique is only used when he talks to his ex-wife (even though he had been shown to be drunk well before he made the call), suggesting it reflects not just his drunken stupor but also his distress when he fails to reconnect with her. The scene also features discontinuous editing (editing that overtly calls attention to itself), jumping back and forth between snippets of the call and instances of his increasingly erratic behavior at the table, mirroring his bewilderment when he realizes the relationship with his ex-wife is beyond repair. The compounding of all of these techniques ensures the sporadic blurriness seen during the call is seen as an expressive visualization of his emotional and physical state at this moment, and not a technical error by the filmmakers. Fittingly, the shot at the end of the call (bottom right) keeps the phone in sharp focus and shows him gradually entering an area of blurriness as he heads back to the table, symbolizing the uncertainty he faces after losing any hope of mending his marriage.

The Constant Gardener, Fernando Meirelles, Director; César Charlone, Cinematographer, 2005

Most viewers are not consciously aware how lenses impact the look of the images they see on the screen, but after years of watching movies they are familiar with the various cinematic "lens aesthetics" that are part of the visual language of movies. For instance, the unnatural compression of perspective seen when using long telephoto lenses is not distracting or jarring to audiences, even though the only times they would experience this effect in everyday life (outside of a movie) would be while looking through a telescope or a pair of binoculars. Likewise, the blurry backgrounds often used in character close-ups is so well established that showing one of these shots with a sharp background can readily communicate something unusual is taking place (the *Tension* section of this chapter includes an example of this technique). This familiarity with cinematic aesthetics is routinely exploited by filmmakers when they want to suggest that something of an incongruous or even disturbing nature is happening, by introducing unconventional imagery that audiences are not used to seeing. Specialized lenses can be particularly helpful in these situations, because they tend to produce images with unusual visual qualities in terms of magnification, focusing, and optical distortion. Among these, the tilt-shift lens, with its ability to have only a section of the focusing plane in sharp focus (the position of which can be shifted mid-recording), can be an ideal tool to communicate a sense of instability and tension, especially when combined with other techniques that also result in unorthodox images, like unbalanced framing, unmotivated camera movement, and distorting focal lengths.

The Constant Gardener, Fernando Meirelles' film adaptation of John le Carré's novel by the same name, uses a tilt-shift lens at a critical juncture to visualize the trepidation and nervousness a character experiences as he is about to go past the "point of no return". When Justin Quayle (Ralph Fiennes), a timid British diplomat stationed in Kenya discovers that his wife Tessa, an Amnesty International activist, is found dead under suspicious circumstances, he sets out to uncover the truth behind her murder. During his investigation, he learns she may have uncovered evidence of illegal drug trials and massive malpractice by a powerful pharmaceutical corporation working in collusion with high-ranking British government officials. He is savagely beaten and warned he will suffer the same fate as his wife if he does not stop his inquiries, but he ignores the threats and flies back to Kenya to locate a doctor who holds key incriminating evidence. His arrival at Nairobi's airport is shown in a tight close-up, taken with a tilt-shift lens that maintains only a portion of his battered face in sharp focus, reflecting his anxiousness as he is questioned about the reasons for his visit by a customs official (left page, top left frame). A handheld camera that at times crops him from the frame complements the unusual look of the tilt-shift lens (bottom right), adding a sense of hesitation and unsteadiness to the image that also randomly shifts the area of focus across his face (top right and bottom frames). An aggressive canted angle further destabilizes the image, visualizing Justin's inner turmoil as he persists in his quest for justice despite knowing he will likely have to pay with his life to gain the information he seeks.

loneliness

Selective focus can help visualize a character's emotional or psychological connection to a physical space, by varying the degree of blurriness used to show it during key moments of a story. If used consistently, this technique can reflect how a specific location makes a character feel: at ease or uncomfortable, safe or exposed, welcome or intimidated. For instance, if a character who is dissatisfied with her job is repeatedly shown with the background out of focus while at work, then the blurriness can signify her dislike of that place, especially if by contrast places where she is seen at ease or happy are consistently shown in sharp focus. One could even show a change in the way a character feels about a place by gradually adjusting the degree of blurriness used to show it, from completely out of focus to tack sharp or vice versa, as long as these looks are applied only in situations that support the meanings assigned to them within the film's image system.

   Elephant, director Gus Van Sant's unsettling drama about a group of high school students in the hours leading up to a shooting spree by two bullied teenagers, features a thoughtful use of selective focus to convey the differing ways they feel about and deal with the social rituals of adolescence while at school. The unconventional narrative structure of this film uses a casual encounter between two students in a hallway to establish a common time frame that connects all of the various story threads; this key moment is used to highlight how Michelle (Kristen Hicks), a girl who is mercilessly bullied and ostracized by her classmates, and Elias (Elias McConnell), an outgoing and popular photog-

raphy student, experience school very differently from each other. In one version of this scene, when Elias walks down a hallway and takes a picture of a classmate (left page, top left frame), his surroundings are shown in sharp focus; for him, school is an inviting place, full of possibilities for social interaction (top right, greeting friends as he arrives to the high school). However, when Michelle walks down the same hallway at the exact same time (Elias can be seen taking the picture we saw him take previously) everything around her is blurry (bottom right); for her, school is an inhospitable place, filled with rejection and scorn (bottom left, being bullied by girls at the gym). In both scenes, the hallway is rendered identically in terms of perspective (shot with an 18mm wide-angle lens[8]), share a similar shot composition, and feature the same dynamic camera move (following the students down the hallway). These carefully planned visual parallels, coupled with the extended duration of both scenes, ensure audiences will notice their drastically different depth of field (achieved by shooting Michelle close to the camera to produce a shallow depth of field, and Elias farther away, resulting in a depth of field that extended from a couple of feet to infinity). However, it is the inclusion of Elias taking a picture from two different perspectives that reveals that the differing looks are motivated by each student's subjective experience of the same moment, suggesting that in Michelle's scene the blurry surroundings visualize her desire to disconnect from the school and the alienation it represents, while the sharp backgrounds in Elias' scene communicate his strong connection to it as a place where he feels safe and accepted

When a technique that overtly stylizes the look of an image is used consistently whenever a certain type of situation takes place in a story, its narrative purpose will be clear and easy to grasp by an audience (as shown in the example from Gus Van Sant's *Elephant* in the previous section). However, it is also possible to use a technique in *different* types of situations within the same story to communicate a much more nuanced and complex idea; this implementation, however, requires a strategic approach to how and when the technique is used, to prevent it from coming across as just a randomly occurring stylization. The meaning of a stylization when used this way is conveyed cumulatively, over the course of an entire narrative, giving the audience enough time between each instance to understand its function in each situation, so that the overall idea being communicated eventually becomes clear.

Julian Schnabel's biographical drama about the final years of Vincent van Gogh's (Willem Dafoe) life at Arles, *At Eternity's Gate*, showcases an unconventional stylization of the image during several pivotal scenes that give audiences a glimpse into his creative process. Schnabel, no stranger to using unorthodox techniques to let audiences experience a character's subjectivity (as seen in his 2007 film *The Diving Bell and the Butterfly*, where a tilt-swing Lensbaby 2.0 is used to emulate the vision of a man waking from a stroke-induced coma), asked his cinematographer Benoît Delhomme to explore the possibility of incorporating the look produced by a pair of antique bifocal sunglasses into the film. Delhomme recreated the bifocal effect by using a split-field diopter attachment on his lenses (mostly 20 and 25mm wide-angles) that overtly blurred the bottom half of the frame at key moments of the film.[9] The effect is showcased in subjective shots that let audiences see things as if through Van Gogh's eyes, often preceded or followed by looking and reaction shots of him that confirm this perspective. The scenes that feature this stylization fall into three main types: moments where van Gogh appears to be enraptured by the beauty of sunlight and nature (left page, top left and right frames), when he is engaged in the process of painting a subject (middle left and right, as he paints Mme. Ginoux [Emmanuelle Seigner] while his friend Paul Gauguin [Oscar Isaac] sketches her), and when he is visibly distressed or feels particularly vulnerable (bottom left and right, during a self-imposed internment in a mental asylum). The systematic implementation of the partially blurred subjective shots in these scenes establishes a strong visual connection that implies they share a common theme: van Gogh's creative process. Interestingly, by including the stylization in scenes where he is psychologically distraught and also in those where he experiences the fervor of artistic expression, it suggests that his precarious mental state was intrinsic to his vision as an artist and the unique way he saw the world. As if to further confirm this connection between his madness and his genius, both of these types of scenes also incorporate a vivid shade of yellow, a color that would dominate much of his work during this stage of his career, either as a naturally occurring part of the environment (middle right), or as a visualization of his altered subjectivity (bottom right).

malevolence

Selective focus techniques are used to direct the audience's attention to a narratively important area of the frame; this is one of the reasons why, for instance, character close-ups routinely feature a blurry background, so that nothing will distract viewers from noticing every detail of an actor's facial expressions. Movie audiences are familiar with this practice, and therefore assume that anything in sharp focus must be inherently meaningful and deserves their attention, and anything out of focus can be safely ignored. However, this convention can be subverted by showing things that would normally be expected to be tack sharp out of focus and vice versa; the resulting images can have an unsettling and even jarring effect, especially when used in situations where audiences expect someone or something important to be revealed (for instance, when introducing key characters, or when showing the outcome of a particularly meaningful event). The effect of this technique can be compounded with thoughtful choices in composition and lighting that further draw attention to what is kept out of focus, adding tension and drama by frustrating the audience's need for clarity and resolution.

A great example of this technique happens in David Fincher's neo-noir crime thriller, *Se7en*, the story of Somerset, a detective on the verge of retirement, and his partner Mills (Brad Pitt), a new arrival set to replace him, as they try to catch a deviously sadistic serial killer before he completes seven ritualistic murders corresponding to the seven deadly sins. Always a step ahead of the detectives because of the meticulous way he plans his murders, the killer, nicknamed John Doe, is finally caught off-guard when they find out where he lives. After stumbling upon the detectives knocking on his door, John Doe flees but is chased by Mills, who ends up getting ambushed in an alley; wounded and unarmed, he finds himself at the mercy of the killer, who stands menacingly before him (left page, bottom frame) while pointing a gun at his temple (top right). This is the first time the audience gets a chance to see John Doe up close; however, his features are concealed throughout the scene, first by showing him in an upside down, silhouetted reflection as he approaches Mills (top left), and then by keeping him completely out of focus and again silhouetted in a shallow depth of field shot that only keeps a portion of the gun in sharp focus. This image not only subverts the audience's expectations for this type of shot and moment in the story by not revealing John Doe's features, but also does it in a way that imbues him with an aura of mystery and almost supernatural evil that reflects the extreme viciousness of his murders. The shot's composition supports these implied character traits, with an extreme low-angle conveying his psychological and physical dominance at this moment, coupled with an aggressively canted angle with strong diagonals in the background that suggest tension and awkwardness. The gun in the foreground takes up almost half of the frame (in a classic implementation of "Hitchcock's Rule"), and is pointed virtually straight at the audience, underlining the impending menace of this moment and its perpetrator. All of these choices, along with the unorthodox use of selective focus, effectively visualize John Doe as an elusive, malevolent entity.

wistfulness

Many of the narrative techniques that involve selective focus have existed for decades (and at least one of them, included in this chapter, is almost 100 years old); others are variations on existing techniques possible thanks to technological innovation (like the use of split-field diopters to simulate deep focus, or using digital means to produce a tilt-shift look). However, one of the remarkable features of cinema as an art form is that its language is continually evolving, not only because of technological innovation, but also because of the way existing techniques can communicate new meanings based on how they are used within the context of each movie. Filmmakers can, in effect, expand the circle of techniques and their meanings with every story they tell. The key is to understand how the narrative connotations of a given technique can be changed so that it is understood in a new way by the audience, which can be done when it is part of a coordinated visual strategy that takes into account the broader image system of a film. This means that the images that precede and follow a technique, as well as the narrative context in which they are presented, can influence an audience to have a completely new interpretation of it, regardless of what its traditional use may have been in other movies.

Set in a fictional Canada where the parents of troubled youths have the power to put them under control of the State without due process, Xavier Dolan's *Mommy* features a remarkable use of selective focus during a particularly poignant sequence leading to the end of the film. After Steve (Antoine-Olivier Pilon), a teenager with severe behavioral issues, is placed back in the custody of his mother, Diane

(Anne Dorval), he turns her life upside down. She enlists the help of a neighbor to home school Steve while she finds ways to make ends meet, but his violent outbursts and an attempted suicide force her to consider surrendering custody of her son to the government. During an outing with the neighbor, Diane daydreams about Steve's future (left page, top left frame), and we see a montage of what she wishes could happen: Steve rectifies his behavior (top right), gets accepted into college and moves out on his own (middle left and right), and gets married in a lavish ceremony (bottom left and right). All of these shots, however, are shown either at various degrees of blurriness from beginning to end, or briefly in focus before they are thrown out of focus. Within the context of the film, the use of out of focus images during Diane's reverie is clear: the idealized future she imagines for Steve is so far removed from the grim reality of their lives that even in her fantasy these images are fleeting, elusive, and undefined. The blurry images in this montage could even suggest Diane's internal conflict regarding Steve's future, as if her maternal instinct wishes the best for her son, prompting the brief moments some images are seen in sharp focus, but deep inside she knows the chances of him changing his ways without professional help are virtually non-existent, visualized by the way the images go blurry almost as soon as they appear. This brilliant use of out of focus imagery to convey such a complex concept is possible because the technique is used only once in the entire film, as well as by the narrative context of the scenes leading up to and following this sequence.

clarity

Advances in technology have made it easier and cheaper than ever to preview the images you are shooting in excellent quality; low-budget filmmakers shooting video no longer have to rely on small, standard definition LCD screens or tiny CRT viewfinders on their cameras to evaluate their shots. Portable external HD monitors with excellent contrast ratios and video resolutions, capable of overlaying digital waveform information, zebras, focus peaking, and 1:1 pixel mapping are cheaper than ever to own or rent, virtually guaranteeing that shots are properly exposed and focused. Unfortunately, these preview tools have also introduced a new habit in some filmmakers: becoming obsessed with checking and re-checking focus during production, unwittingly sacrificing other important aspects of a shot in their quest to get tack-sharp images. While it is expected that at a professional level images should be consistently in focus, sometimes working on a tight schedule can mean getting stuck with a slightly soft focus shot here and there. In fact, soft focus shots are not a rarity, even in the most expensive Hollywood productions; but how is this possible when they have state-of-the art equipment at their disposal and crews famous for their technical excellence? The answer is simple: experienced filmmakers will rarely scrap a shot for being only slightly soft, because they know that story, emotional engagement, and a solid performance trump minor technical flaws every time. If an audience is fully engaged with the plight of the characters in the story, not only they will not mind minor flaws: they will not even notice them. If you have a take that is slightly soft but contains the best performance your actor gave you (even if other takes are perfectly in focus), then *that* is the take that should make the cut.

This principle is illustrated in a wonderful scene from director Spike Jonze's *Adaptation*, the complex story behind Charlie Kaufman's attempt to adapt Susan Orlean's book *The Orchid Thief* to the big screen. As Charlie struggles to come up with a dramatic angle for his screenplay, we learn that Susan (Meryl Streep) has become infatuated with the subject of her novel, John Laroche, a man obsessed with being able to clone an extremely rare orchid. During a late night phone conversation with Laroche while under the psychotropic effects of an orchid extract she snorted, Susan is fascinated by the sound of the dial tone, and asks him to help her recreate it by humming a note; her side of this exchange is covered with a medium close-up that is slightly out of focus, noticeable from the blurred glimmers visible in her eyes (left page, top frame). However, when they manage to perfectly imitate the sound, the shot suddenly turns tack sharp (bottom), as if somehow their achievement brought a moment of clarity and focus to her previously disenchanted life. Cinematographer Lance Acord recalls that the scene was shot under very low light, which made it difficult to assess focus properly, and either he or his focus puller made the adjustment when they realized the shot was slightly soft, without purposely trying to match the precise moment Susan and John managed to replicate the dial tone sound.[10] The magic of this unplanned moment made it to the final cut of the film because story, emotion, and performance prevailed over a slavish concern for technical perfection.

The Duellists. *Ridley Scott, Director; Frank Tidy, Cinematographer. 1977.*

FLARES

Lens flares occur when bright, stray beams of light enter the lens, causing internal reflections between the elements and the diaphragm that result in various types of image degradation, in the form of light streaks, colorful polygonal shapes, fogging of the image, reduced contrast, and desaturated colors. Flares can also obscure subjects from view, and some people think they can pull an audience out of the world of the story because their presence, in effect, reveals the equipment used to record the images on the screen. Filmmakers often use flags, barndoors, matte boxes, eyebrows, lens hoods, and French flags on camera rigs, lenses, and lighting equipment to prevent flares, whether they are shooting indoors or outdoors with natural or artificial light. Advances in modern lens design, construction, and anti-reflective coatings have managed to minimize flares, especially in higher-end lenses; these features are particularly helpful when using short focal lengths (since their larger field of view makes them particularly prone to flaring) and zoom lenses (which tend to produce more noticeable flares because of their many internal elements). However, lens flares can also be an intentional part of the aesthetics of a shot. Beginning in the late 1960s, a handful of pioneering filmmakers developed a visual style that incorporated lens flares into their storytelling approach. The influences for creatively employing what was originally considered to be a technical flaw came from a number of places: European filmmakers who experimented with new narrative and production modes, documentary cinéma-vérité shooting techniques made possible by advances in portable filmmaking equipment and lenses, and the work of experimental filmmakers who tested, pushed, and subverted every aspect of the visual language and image production. As lens flares became more widely used in narrative and documentary filmmaking, they were eventually integrated into the visual vocabulary of mainstream movies, and narrative conventions developed around their use. Today, lens flares have become so mainstream that companies like ARRI and Cooke offer uncoated front and rear elements for some of their cinema lenses, giving filmmakers an extra level of control over the look of their flares.

Director Ridley Scott's first feature film, *The Duellists*, ends with a lens flare shot that while unconventional for an 18th-century period drama, is nevertheless visually stunning and narratively brilliant. Thematically and formally evocative of Stanley Kubrick's *Barry Lyndon*, *The Duellists* tells the story of Lieutenant Feraud (Harvey Keitel), a Bonapartist from lower-class origins who spends fifteen years engaged in a series of duels against Lieutenant D'Hubert, an aristocrat who accommodates him only because their code of honor demands it. During their last duel, D'Hubert gets the chance to kill Feraud but instead forces him to accept defeat and never confront him again. Afterwards, a despondent Feraud stands on a bluff looking over a vast landscape as the setting sun peeks from behind a cloud, creating a stream of colorful lens flares that dominate the frame (left page). The painterly beauty of the composition (reminiscent of period art depicting Napoleon's final exile to St. Helena) is enhanced by the gradual appearance of the flares, which underscore the approaching sunset, and symbolically suggest the end of the Napoleonic era and its ideal of equality between the classes, the driving force behind Feraud's relentless quest to prove his worth against D'Hubert. Scott, a brilliant visualist well known for the polished imagery of his films, integrated lens flares in this scene in a way that beautifully emblematizes a central theme of *The Duellists* in a single, memorable shot.

The Hobbit: An Unexpected Journey. *Peter Jackson, Director; Andrew Lesnie, Cinematographer. 2012 (top).*
Kung Fu Hustle. *Stephen Chow, Director; Hang-Sang Poon, Cinematographer. 2004 (bottom left).*
Gore Verbinski, Director; Roger Deakins, Visual Consultant. 2011 (bottom right).

One of the classic uses of lens flares is to suggest a character possesses superior physical, psychological, and even supernatural qualities, in what are known commonly as "hero shots". In these images, usually taken from a slight low-angle to imply power, a character adopts a confident posture, as a dynamic camera (dolly-ins and dolly arcs around a subject are common) reveals strong lens flares that appear to emanate directly from their bodies, symbolizing their actual or perceived power according to the narrative context. In some cases, lens flares are incorporated to such a degree that they obscure a character from view, silhouetting them and forming an aura effect that can imply spiritual and even divine attributes. These shots are often featured after a character accomplishes a particularly difficult task or overcomes an extraordinary challenge, and are sometimes accompanied by narration and an epic, triumphant music cue that further contextualizes their depiction as a heroic figure. This lens flare technique has transcended language and cultural boundaries, and can be found in movies from virtually any national cinema and genre.

Peter Jackson's *The Hobbit: An Unexpected Journey* (left page, top frame) showcases a classic use of lens flares in a hero shot during a flashback sequence, as a narration recounts the story of how Thorin (Richard Armitage) rallied his troops and turned the tide against the Orcs when he defeated his nemesis, Azog. The flashback culminates with a heavily flared shot of Thorin as the camera circles around him from a low-angle while he stands victorious over a field littered with his fallen troops. Every aspect of this shot is de-

signed to create a strong, iconic image of Thorin as a classical hero, capped off with photorealistic computer-generated lens flares added in postproduction.

Kung Fu Hustle, Stephen Chow's period comedy spoofing martial arts films, uses lens flares in a hero shot toward the end of the film, when Sing (Stephen Chow) offers to teach his vanquished enemy the martial art technique he used to defeat him. The villain is shocked by Sing's magnanimous gesture, who at this moment is shown in a low-angle medium close-up with the sun shining behind his head and heavy lens flares covering his face (bottom left). In this narrative and cultural context, the lens flares are not just meant to show Sing as a classical hero, but also to imply he has a connection to the heavens and the divine order they symbolize in Buddhism (just moments before he is shown being blessed by a cloud formation in the shape of a Buddha figure).

Advancements in computer-generated animation have reached a level of photorealism that allow the creation of lens flare effects virtually identical to the real thing, as seen in this classic hero shot from the ending of Gore Verbinski's *Rango*, a comedy that parodies the western genre (bottom right). In it, the title character (voiced and performed by Johnny Depp) delivers a cliché-ridden speech singing his own overinflated praises as he is bathed in the lens flares of a setting sun and the "camera" slowly dollies in while triumphant music plays on the soundtrack. Before he can finish, he is thrown from his saddle, appropriately subverting the convention in a parody of the classic hero shot.

atmosphere

One of the earliest expressive uses of lens flares in mainstream filmmaking was to visualize the sun's oppressive heat, a convention that continues to be used to this day. However, when *Cool Hand Luke*'s director Stuart Rosenberg and cinematographer Conrad L. Hall first wanted to use lens flares for this purpose, they faced stern opposition from their studio, which considered them an imperfection that did not belong in a major motion picture.[11] The cinematographic conventions of the time were strictly aimed at the creation of technically flawless, meticulously lit and composed images, often at the expense of the spatial and/or lighting circumstances that would logically exist in a real-life location, prioritizing a highly polished aesthetic over verisimilitude. Thankfully, Rosenberg and Hall prevailed, and in the process expanded the cinematic vocabulary by pioneering an aesthetic that incorporated technical imperfections to express a more believable reality. This new style of cinematography would resonate with audiences familiar with the sometimes technically rough imagery of cinéma-vérité documentaries (from directors like D.A. Pennebaker, Frederick Wiseman, and the Maysles Brothers, to name just a few), and with the work of maverick filmmakers who were seeking a visual language that would advance the cultural, political, and social changes of their era by challenging traditional Hollywood production modes.

 Cool Hand Luke, the story of a rebellious war veteran who is sentenced to spend time on a Florida chain gang after destroying a row of parking meters, features two early examples of an expressive use of lens flares, designed to convey the harsh conditions under which convicts are forced to work. Early in the film, the prison is established as a brutal and inhumane place, run by a sadistic warden who enjoys inflicting physical and psychological abuse on inmates under the watchful gaze of Boss Godfrey (Morgan Woodward), a malevolent prison officer who always wears menacing mirrored sunglasses. When we first see the chain gang doing road work, Boss Godfrey makes an entrance designed for maximum dramatic effect; the shot begins by showing only his shoes in a low-angle medium close-up that zooms out to a medium long shot as he emerges from behind a truck. At this precise moment, a prominent lens flare crosses the frame diagonally, moving with the camera as it pans to follow him. The flare adds a visual punch to the character's reveal, and associates him with the sun's oppressive heat (left page, top frame). Immediately afterwards, "Tramp" (Harry Dean Stanton), one of the inmates working on the road, is shown in a medium close-up that juxtaposes him against the early morning sun and a large orange flare; he is suddenly overcome by the extreme heat in a manner that makes it look as if the lens flare itself knocks him down (bottom). In these examples, the inclusion of flares is justified by the natural conditions present in the location, but they also have the clear narrative function of visualizing the overbearing heat of the sun, underscoring its dramatic impact in this scene and the story. This may explain why *Cool Hand Luke*'s lens flares have become legendary, even though there are only two clear examples where they are used for this purpose out of the many road work scenes featured in the film.

ambiguity

Lens flares can make a bold visual statement and overtly stylize the look of a shot; because of this, most filmmakers try to keep their use to a minimum, lest their inclusion becomes so distracting it pulls the audience out of the story. However, if flares are justified by a narrative context and are part of a consistent visual strategy that makes their meaning clear (through thoughtful choices in lighting, shot composition, and editing style, among others), it is possible to use them repeatedly throughout a film; when featured this way, they can suggest a range of ideas and meanings without the risk of being seen as merely a visual flourish for its own sake.

Dennis Hopper's *Easy Rider*, a film that marked the advent of the independent American film as a commercially viable venture, is also among the first high-profile films to include an informed, creative, and narratively consistent use of lens flares. The film follows two hippie bikers, Wyatt (Peter Fonda) and Billy (Dennis Hopper), as they travel across America after a successful drug deal. During their journey, they meet a broad cross-section of American society, from respected authority figures to social outcasts. At times, Hopper seems to romanticize the American counterculture movement of the 1960s, while at others he imbues it with a sense of melancholy and hopelessness; this central ambiguity is reflected in the film's visual style, and particularly in the way lens flares are used throughout. For instance, several montages of Wyatt and Billy riding their bikes in the open highway feature conspicuous lens flares (left page, top frame) that are allowed to dominate the frame in a way that was considered unacceptable by contemporary Hollywood

standards, but is consistent with *Easy Rider*'s transgressions of classical narrative conventions (a fragmented, episodic structure, use of jump cuts, staccato editing, and mix of film formats and visual styles). Lens flares in these sequences also help convey the thrill of riding a chopper on a sunny day against the majestic natural beauty of iconic American landscapes, idealizing Wyatt and Billy's journey and their lifestyle. Lens flares are also at times used purely for their aesthetic qualities, as shown during a scene when Wyatt wanders through a dilapidated shack at the side of a highway (bottom left), which features large sun flares streaming through the exposed beams of a roof intercut with shots of his gaze, suggesting a special connection that is left unexplained. Later, when Wyatt and Billy get high on LSD while visiting a cemetery with a couple of prostitutes, aggressive lens flares visualize their drug-distorted perspective. Their hallucinatory subjectivity is further complemented with grainy 16mm film stock, shaky handheld camera work, distorting fisheye lenses, and wayward focusing (bottom right). The resulting imagery does not depict their hallucinogenic episode as a mind-expanding, transcendent experience, but rather as a harrowing, nightmarish vision where their fears and insecurities are exposed and a sense of despair prevails. *Easy Rider* is one of the first films to widely incorporate lens flares following their introduction in Stuart Rosenberg's *Cool Hand Luke*, and it did so with creativity, variety, and narrative sophistication. Virtually all of the storytelling applications of lens flares seen in this film would eventually become visual tropes in mainstream and independent filmmaking.

There are many different kinds of lens flares and as many ways to control their size, shape, number, and intensity. For instance, an f-stop setting can be selected not for a lens' sweet spot or a desired depth of field, but for how it will impact the size and shape of a flare; likewise, one could purposely choose to use a set of older lenses with worn-out anti-reflective coatings (or even no coatings at all) to create more noticeable flares, which are harder to produce with modern, technically superior glass. Although in most cases prime lenses are preferred over zooms, the latter might be a better choice if more numerous flares are needed, and one could even pick a lens for a particular shot because of the number of blades in its iris, to create a flare of a certain shape. When every detail of the look of lens flares is deliberate, they can communicate narrative meaning beyond aesthetic considerations, and can even be a central element of a visual strategy, supporting the story's core idea or theme.

Lens flares play a key role and are a recurring visual theme in director Iain Softley's *K-PAX*, the story of Prot (Kevin Spacey) a man who claims to have extraterrestrial origins and the capability of intergalactic travel using only beams of light, and the psychiatrist in charge of treating him, Dr. Powell. As Dr. Powell digs into his patient's past to uncover the truth behind his claims, Prot's extraordinary knowledge of astrophysics and uncanny influence over patients in his ward make his story increasingly believable, leading the doctor to reevaluate his professional and personal life in the process. The film features a broad variety of flares, integrated into the narrative in ways that at times seem to support Prot's alien provenance, while at other times suggesting a more plausible explanation for his strange behavior. Our first glimpse of Prot, for instance, implies he materializes in the middle of Grand Central Terminal via a beam of light that produces large flares across the frame (left page, top left and right frames). Likewise, a crystal paperweight in Dr. Powell's office produces stylized patterns of multicolor flares during regression therapy sessions with Prot, as if his presence has the power to somehow alter the physics of light (middle left). The sunrise on the day Prot is set to depart for K-PAX (his planet's purported name) also displays unusual-looking flares that are complemented with a strangely vivid, purplish sky that suggests something out of the ordinary is about to take place (middle right). When Prot is invited to a picnic in Dr. Powell's house, at one point he is shown in a dramatic low-angle shot that juxtaposes him against a powerful sun flare (bottom left), momentarily visualizing the special relationship with light and celestial bodies he claims to have (also a visual trope that can suggest spiritual or divine attributes). However, when Dr. Powell uncovers details of a terrible tragedy from Prot's past while visiting his former home, a similar sun flare is shown, implying that there could be a more earthly explanation for his fixation with light. The various looks of the flares throughout the film, created in-camera without the aid of CGI and always motivated by natural light,[12] consistently visualize the film's central ambiguity regarding Prot's true identity, ultimately hinting at the possibility that in some cases the fantastic and the mundane may not always be mutually exclusive.

Close Encounters of the Third Kind. Steven Spielberg, Director: Vilmos Zsigmond, Cinematographer. 1977.

mystery

When used thoughtfully, lens flares can be a lot more than a peripheral visual element; they can be integral to the visual strategy of a film, helping to convey tone or mood, suggesting concrete or symbolic traits in a character, and even become character-like themselves.

A superlative example of an expressive use of lens flares can be seen throughout director Steven Spielberg's *Close Encounters of the Third Kind*, a film that traces the journey of suburban everyman Roy Neary after he has an encounter with a UFO that compels him to investigate the truth behind his experience. Spielberg meticulously develops an aura of mystery around the UFOs, never showing them in full detail until the very end of the film, relying instead on the power of suggestion and subtext (a technique he refined to maximum effect in his 1975 blockbuster, *Jaws*). Rather than shown explicitly, UFOs are instead represented as dark shapes that are always obscured by lens flares produced by their bright, multicolored lights, strategically arranged in patterns that at times anthropomorphize them (left page, top frame). Lens flares are featured prominently in every one of the "close encounters", conveying the UFOs' otherworldly nature by their unusual appearance and behavior, while also imbuing them with distinct personalities as they glide silently and effortlessly through the night skies of Indiana. Flares are also used to suggest the tremendous power of the aliens' advanced technology, shown when UFOs appear to scan their surroundings with powerful beams of light that recall the "tractor beams" often described and illustrated in alien abduction stories (bottom left). When the aliens

are finally shown, their appearance, like the UFOs, is also partially concealed by highly stylized lens flares of various shapes, colors, and sizes that leave much to the imagination of viewers regarding their true form, while giving them a supernatural aura with quasi-divine undertones (bottom right). Spielberg's use of lens flares is so consistent throughout the film that it is hard to find them in any scene not involving the UFOs or the aliens; this establishes a strong visual connection between them that he cleverly exploits in a scene where alien encounter hopefuls (and the audience) are led to mistake an army helicopter equipped with search lights for an alien craft. This type of misdirection would not have been possible without a well thought-out visual strategy and image system in place behind the depiction of the aliens and their ships; much of the mystery and awe generated by the lens flares would have been diluted if they had been used excessively or inconsistently. Although Spielberg's use of lens flares in *Close Encounters* is deeply woven into the narrative as a way to visualize the mysterious nature of the aliens and their ships, they also function to create the illusion that the UFOs and the human characters inhabit the same physical space in shots where they share the frame, adding a critical sense of verisimilitude to the alien ships (actually small models equipped with tiny lights, created by Douglas Trumbull). While visual effects of the type used in *Close Encounters* are rarely used in modern filmmaking, its innovative lens flare techniques have become popular again, this time to disguise the over-polished and sometimes artificial look of computer-generated effects.

physicality

One of the main reasons many filmmakers tend to avoid lens flares is that they can call attention to the filmmaking apparatus itself, potentially distracting an audience from the story. The presence of lens flares implies the presence of a lens and a camera that can dispel the illusion that a viewer is experiencing the events they are watching first hand and not through the artifice of the film production process. This implied physical aspect of flares, however, can be used as part of a narrative strategy, in situations where it is necessary to imbue an event (be it real or computer generated) with an aura of believability and physical reality.

J.J. Abrams' reboot of the Star Trek franchise, *Star Trek*, showcases examples of virtually every kind of lens flare (including anamorphic flares, light streaks, diaphragm reflections, and haloes) in virtually every major sequence of the film, be it live action or wholly computer generated. Whether created practically on location (by aiming a powerful flashlight into the lens while checking a preview monitor to precisely control their appearance and location within the frame) or added digitally during postproduction, the flares are made to look and behave exactly like the unintended flares often seen in documentary films, at times obscuring large, narratively important sections of the image (left page, top frame). Their realistic behavior and appearance add a patina of physicality and believability to the numerous virtual sets and CGI set pieces used throughout the film (bottom left, right), providing a unified aesthetic to seamlessly integrate these virtual elements and environments with the live-action segments. This lens flare aesthetic is a departure from their more conventional use in mainstream films, where they are positioned unobtrusively in the frame and manipulated to look visually pleasing, focusing almost exclusively on their aesthetic value while often ignoring any potential narrative function they may offer. In an age where audiences expect photorealistic perfection in the visual effects of a film, particularly in the science-fiction genre, the innovative use of lens flares in *Star Trek* delivered just that, by cleverly incorporating what is commonly considered a technical flaw as a key element of its visual strategy. Abrams' use of lens flares was not universally well received, however; critics felt they were overused, too obtrusive, and generally distracting. While these complaints may be at least partially justified, there is no denying that Abrams' creative integration of lens flares was responsible for popularizing the notion of a "flare aesthetic" in the mainstream consciousness, and it may have also influenced more than a few software companies to create applications that can generate virtually any kind of lens flare imaginable, for devices ranging from desktops to smartphones and anything in between. Anamorphic lens flares in particular have become especially popular, prompting a growing aftermarket of used anamorphic projector lenses and adapters, aimed at DSLR filmmakers who want to incorporate the "anamorphic lens flare look" to their projects. Although the use of lens flares in Abrams' *Star Trek* may have been excessive at times, thus diluting some of their narrative potential, their prominent inclusion in such a high-profile movie undeniably revived interest in their visual storytelling possibilities.

attachment

Lens flares can make a powerful statement about a character when used sparingly and in situations where their intended meaning is clear, so their inclusion is not misunderstood as being a purely aesthetic choice by the filmmaker. For instance, using a strong lens flare in a shot of a character immediately after they complete a difficult task or overcome a major challenge can make them seem courageous, powerful, and even heroic (as shown in the examples in the *Prowess* section of this chapter). However, if flares are used indiscriminately throughout a film, they can lose their ability to convey character attributes, even when included at important junctures of a narrative: their expressive potential will be effectively diluted by overuse. Just as important as the narrative context in which lens flares are presented and the frequency of their use is their placement within the image system of a story, meaning their actual location in the sequence of events. There are moments in almost every film that are inherently meaningful by virtue of *when* they occur, such as the opening and closing images, or the first and last time a main character or an important location is seen, among others. Often, filmmakers like to underline connections between these key moments to showcase character growth and/or change, by using shots designed to make a vivid impression in the minds of the audience so they can be easily recalled when they reappear or a similar image is shown. The overt stylization lens flares can add to the look of a shot can be instrumental in creating these visual connections, especially when their use is restricted to images meant for this purpose within a story.

Thomas Vinterberg's *Far from the Madding Crowd*, based on Thomas Hardy's novel by the same name, demonstrates the value of using flares strategically for maximum effect, by featuring them prominently at two key moments of the film to foreground the connection that gradually develops between a shepherd, Gabriel Oak (Matthias Schoenaerts), and his employer, Bathsheba Everdene (Carey Mulligan). The very first time Gabriel is seen (barely two minutes into the film) he is shown in a low-angle medium close-up shot with a strong sun flare directly above his head (left page, top frame), in a composition that is visually evocative of the classic "hero shot". At this point in the film, however, no narrative evidence has been provided to establish him as heroic or courageous, so the flare can only suggest these traits, and instead serves to overtly stylize Gabriel's introduction while creating a strong visual connection between him and his bucolic surroundings. Lens flares are not used again in this way in the entire film until the last scene, when Bathsheba finally agrees to marry him (bottom), shown in a low-angle medium close-up two shot that closely resembles the composition of our first image of him, with a strong sun flare placed directly between them. The flare in this shot serves the dual purpose of signaling that the story has come full circle by visually recalling the opening of the film (a point reinforced by the nearly identical location and the repetition of the musical theme heard during Gabriel's introduction), and links Bathsheba with the same overt stylization the audience associates with Gabriel, visualizing the mutual emotional attachment they share at this pivotal moment of the narrative.

2001: A Space Odyssey. *Stanley Kubrick, Director; Geoffrey Unsworth, Cinematographer, 1968.*

DISTORTION

There are two main types of distortion produced by lenses: perspective distortion, or the apparent compression or expansion of distances along the z-axis of the frame, and optical distortion, when lenses show physically straight lines as slight curves (also known as curvilinear distortion). This chapter explores the expressive application of optical distortion, hereafter referred to simply as "distortion", (perspective distortion is discussed in the *Space* chapter). Filmmakers usually prefer to avoid overt distortion, especially when shooting close-ups of actors' faces, because it can exaggerate facial features in an unflattering way. In long and extreme long shots, typically when showcasing landscapes and/or in establishing shots, distortion can also visibly deform objects located near the edges of the frame in unnatural ways. Some directors and cinematographers, however, understand that in the right context distortion can be a powerfully expressive tool to visualize a thematic, psychological, dramatic, and even a philosophical view of a situation, a character, or even a location. Distortion should therefore not be automatically dismissed, but instead considered for what it can offer to serve the storytelling needs of your film; in fact, distortion can even be *the* central aesthetic and narrative principle that informs and influences every aspect of a visual strategy. When deciding how much distortion to use on an image, it is important to take into account that the perception of its effect by an audience will depend on how it fits within your film's image system, particularly in relation to the way it was used in other shots. A wildly distorted image, for instance, will lose much of its visual impact if most of the film is shot using similarly distorting focal lengths; conversely, if mostly normal lenses are used, the effect of a shot with even slight distortion will be quite noticeable to an audience. With this in mind, you could use distortion in varying degrees strategically throughout a film, depending on how subtle or overt the resulting effect needs to be. If distortion is used consistently, you can control not only how it affects the aesthetics of your images, but also its narrative impact and meaning to an audience.

A sophisticated example of using extreme distortion to visualize and comment on a character's subjectivity can be seen in Stanley Kubrick's *2001: A Space Odyssey*, a film that posits that extraterrestrial life was responsible for the inception of human intelligence. After discovering a mysterious monolith on the Moon, a spaceship is sent to Jupiter to investigate its origins; during this journey, HAL 9000, a computer designed to mimic human behavior in charge of running the ship, appears to malfunction, prompting astronauts Frank Poole (Gary Lockwood) and Dave Bowman (Keir Dullea) to question its reliability. HAL's subjectivity is represented throughout the film with a fisheye lens (there is some debate whether it was a 160° Cinerama Fairchild-Curtis or a more conventional wide-angle) that produces an extremely distorted perspective (left page), seemingly reflecting not just his actual field of view, but also his warped, unnatural view of humans and their affairs. The distorting effect is compounded by the lens' aggressive vignetting, which adds a voyeuristic aspect to HAL's presence that is nevertheless justified since he is shown to have only one protruding lens "eye", and therefore lacks human-like stereoscopic and peripheral vision. The aesthetics of the fisheye lens used to portray HAL's subjectivity suggest that although he may sound and act like a human being, his true nature is far removed from the human experience, presaging the deadly conflict that would arise between human and artificial intelligence in this film.

Fear and Loathing in Las Vegas, Terry Gilliam. Director; Nicola Pecorini, Cinematographer, 1998.

surreality

Lenses in the "normal" range are generally believed to approximate human vision and are fairly neutral in terms of distortion. Because of this, filmmakers rely on them when they want to avoid overtly changing perspective, rate of movement, and the look of facial features. However, the aesthetics of what we consider a "normal" focal length are relative, and should not be thought of as being confined to a specific measurement or range. In fact, any focal length can be designated as normal within a particular project if used consistently. For instance, if a 28mm wide-angle is used for most of the shots in a film, it would effectively become the normal lens in that story's image system, and suddenly switching to a 50mm would have the equivalent visual impact of using a telephoto lens. The key is to use whichever focal length is selected as normal predominantly, so that even a slight deviation from it will result in a noticeable change. It is important to consider, however, that redefining what a normal lens is will impact every aspect of a production, from lighting to art direction and even the blocking of actors; this is why lens selections must be discussed early in the preproduction process, and not be something that gets decided on the day of the shoot. The visual style of a film should also be developed taking into account the optical characteristics of whichever lens is selected as normal, from the way it may distort perspective and facial features, to its effect on movement within the frame. Ignoring these factors runs the risk of producing ambiguous and/or narratively indifferent images that can obfuscate and may even contradict the themes, subtext, and core ideas of a story.

A filmmaker who has mastered a unique look by routinely redefining what is considered normal (literally in respect to the focal lengths he uses, and figuratively in his films) is director Terry Gilliam, who developed a signature visual style using almost exclusively wide-angle lenses. Combined with canted angle shots, close-ups that overtly distort facial features, and wide shots with deep depths of field, Gilliam's style is also famous for its visually dense, detailed mise en scène and art direction as well as an affinity for surreal stories and characters. Gilliam's *Fear and Loathing in Las Vegas*, an adaptation of Hunter S. Thompson's novel by the same name, is emblematic of his visual style, which is particularly well suited to convey the paranoid, drug-induced, psychedelic journey taken by journalist Raoul Duke (Johnny Depp) and his lawyer Dr. Gonzo (Benicio Del Toro) as they search for the "American Dream" while covering a Las Vegas motorcycle race. Almost the entire film was shot with wide-angle lenses and canted shots, resulting in wildly distorted visuals that match the excesses perpetrated by the duo (left page, top and bottom left frames). A notable exception, however, happens near the mid-point of the film, where an uncharacteristically sober and lucid Duke ponders that the hippie and counterculture movements' promise of social change and attempt to redefine the meaning of the American Dream had failed (bottom right). This bittersweet, somber moment was shot with a more conventional normal range focal length that (ironically) makes it feel unsettling and incongruous with the rest of the film, appropriately shifting the tone to reflect the heartbreaking disappointment felt by this character.

Amélie. Jean-Pierre Jeunet, Director; Bruno Delbonnel, Cinematographer. 2001.
Thérèse. Claude Miller, Director; Gérard de Battista, Cinematographer. 2012.

whimsy

Although overtly distorting focal lengths are ideal to suggest characters and the world they inhabit are abnormal, surreal, or operate under a distorted set of values (a usage examined in *Fear and Loathing in Las Vegas* in the previous section), they can also imply more positive traits, provided they are part of a well thought-out visual strategy. The key is not to think about distortion solely in terms of its potential negative impact, or to focus solely on how it can alter facial features in an unflattering way, but to also consider how it can complement the look of your characters and even your locations. Portrait photographers are keenly aware of this concept, and routinely use distorting focal lengths when they want to enhance or conceal physical features based on their subject's facial characteristics. With the right combination of lighting choices and shooting angles, even wildly distorting focal lengths can make characters look likeable, comical, attractive, and anything in between, as required by the story. Likewise, overt distortion can make locations look inviting, cozy, and even magical, by carefully pairing it with art direction choices, lighting, and shot compositions that selectively emphasize some physical aspects while minimizing others.

Jean-Pierre Jeunet's romantic comedy *Amélie*, the story of Amélie Poulain (Audrey Tautou), an eccentric young Parisian girl who one day decides to surreptitiously involve herself in the lives of friends and strangers in her neighborhood, illustrates the use of overt distortion to establish the general tone of a narrative. The careful attention paid to every aspect of *Amélie*'s art direction, lighting, blocking, make-up, and costume design also extended to their lens selection, which involved director Jean-Pierre Jeunet and cinematographer Bruno Delbonnel assigning specific focal lengths to actors after considering their unique facial characteristics. For the lead character of Amélie, they chose 25mm and 27mm wide-angle lenses combined with precise blocking (her head tilted slightly forward and close enough to the lens to accentuate barrel distortion) and shot compositions that exaggerated her facial features (slight high-angles to magnify the size of her eyes and make her body look tiny).[13] The frame grabs on the opposite page (top, bottom left and middle), taken from key moments throughout the film, show how consistently the same framing and level of facial distortion were used for Amélie's close-up shots. Far from making her look unattractive, however, the wide-angle distortion gives her a slightly comical, cartoonish look that perfectly complements *Amélie*'s heavily saturated color palette, droll production design, ebullient soundtrack, omniscient narration, and unabashedly charming story to set a whimsical tone not unlike that of a fairy tale. In contrast, note Audrey Tautou's dramatically different appearance in director Claude Miller's film *Thérèse* (bottom right), a drama about an unhappily married woman driven to commit a crime; this shot was taken with a lens closer to a normal focal length and uses a more conventional shot composition. Interestingly, when juxtaposed with the shots from *Amélie*, the shot from *Thérèse* feels out of place even though it features the least amount of distortion, illustrating how easy it is to redefine what is considered a normal focal length (as examined in the previous section).

The Girl with the Dragon Tattoo, David Fincher, Director; Jeff Cronenweth, Cinematographer, 2011

intimidation

When used thoughtfully, lens distortion can be combined to communicate a character's subjectivity, which is an effective way to draw a viewer into the story during moments where a heightened level of engagement is desired. One technique involves establishing the general look of a scene using lenses within the normal focal length range, and then switching to a more distorting focal length at a point when the audience is meant to experience events from the physical, emotional, or psychological perspective of a particular character. The visual impact of this technique can be overt or subtle, depending on how pronounced the focal length shift is; for example, if a shot taken with a slight wide-angle is preceded by shots taken with a normal lens, the change will stand out without being too obvious, but using an extreme wide-angle after using longer lenses will produce a more noticeable, jarring change. A common variation involves using short focal lengths to reflect an altered physical or mental state in a character, with the level of optical or perspective distortion applied in direct proportion to how abnormal their perception is supposed to be; alternatively, it is also possible to use a normal lens to convey an altered state, if wide-angles or telephotos are used predominantly beforehand, though this is less frequently done (as seen in director Terry Gilliam's *Fear and Loathing in Las Vegas*, examined on page 153).

Director David Fincher's *The Girl with the Dragon Tattoo* has a classic use of this technique in a pivotal scene where Lisbeth Salander (Rooney Mara), an anti–social outcast with extraordinary computer hacking skills, exacts revenge on Nils (Yorick van Wageningen), a state guardian who abuses his position to sexually assault her. Using her knowledge of surveillance technology, she arranges to secretly record her abuser during one of his attacks. After she obtains this damning evidence, she tricks him into meeting her again, where she turns the tables and brutally tortures him. During this assault, she asks him: "Do you doubt what's on those reports that have followed me all my life? What do they say? They say I'm insane." The film then cuts to a close-up of Lisbeth as she tells him: "It's true, *I am insane*", (left page, top frame). This shot, taken with a lens with a significantly shorter focal length than what was used earlier (bottom right and left), overtly distorts Lisbeth's face because of her close proximity to the camera, lending a disturbing credibility to her statement. The effect is accentuated by the use of a shallow depth of field (created in part by the short focusing distance) that blurs everything except her distorted facial features. The slight underlighting and the unbalanced diagonal lines formed by the ceiling in the background also contribute to the unnerving quality of this moment, but her staring directly into the lens from a threatening high-angle makes it even more jarring. By using a subjective shot when she declares her insanity, audiences are allowed to experience this moment as if through the eyes of the tortured guardian, effectively placing *them* as the recipients of Lisbeth's wrath. The use of the wide-angle's distortion in this particular shot is primarily conveying the intense intimidation felt by her guardian, who is facing psychopathic insanity face-to-face at this moment, while simultaneously visualizing Lisbeth's darkest character.

equiem for a Dream. *Darren Aronofsky, Director; Matthew Libatique, Cinematographer, 2000.*

The barrel distortion of wide-angle lenses with very short focal lengths can produce wildly misshapen facial features that are more noticeable than the pincushion distortion of long telephoto lenses. This is because wide-angle lenses, with their much wider field of view, require a shorter camera to subject distance to frame a close-up, allowing facial features to be warped by the expansion of perspective and, if close enough, optical distortion (see page 41 for examples of this effect). Choosing a wide-angle lens when one purposely wants to distort facial features, however, is only the first step. As with other techniques, every detail matters: how much distortion is necessary? What specific focal length will produce it? Should you use a standard or a cinema lens? These considerations are important, because all lenses are constructed and designed differently and have their own individual "optical personality"; two different lenses with the same focal length can produce noticeably different images in terms of color bias, contrast, sharpness, aberrations, vignetting, flares, and distortion. The best lens for the job may not always be the most expensive, or the fastest, or the more advanced in its design, since they may not be well suited to produce the kind of distortion a cheaper or older lens may provide; this is why cinematographers do a lot of testing when they need to assess the optical characteristics of a lens intended for a special purpose.

Darren Aronofsky's *Requiem for a Dream* uses extreme barrel distortion to visualize the altered, drug-induced subjectivity of Sara Goldfarb (Ellen Burstyn), an elderly woman who gets hooked on diet pills while trying to lose weight before appearing in an infomercial. Using a wide-angle lens to convey the perspective of someone under the influence of drugs is not unusual, but the particular way it is implemented in this scene exemplifies the attention to detail that allows a filmmaker to fully exploit the expressive potential of a lens. Every aspect of this scene, from shot composition to the blocking and even sound design, was orchestrated to foreground the distortion effect as much as possible. Sara's close proximity to the camera at the beginning of the shot (left page, top frame), for instance, produces a maximum level of distortion of her facial features, while still keeping her within an area of acceptable focus (bottom). The shot was also carefully composed so that her face would be close to an edge of the frame, where the lens' barrel distortion is most pronounced for this focal length; if she had been even just a little closer to the center, the effect would not have been as severe. The soundtrack complements the overt use of the optical distortion, featuring a loud, crashing sound right as she turns to face the camera, underlining the visual impact of her grotesquely distorted features. In addition to these techniques, the frame rate was also digitally altered: it is initially slowed down and then suddenly sped up, making the visual and aural manipulations of the scene even more jarring. The overt stylization of this shot effectively communicates Sara's distorted perception because the filmmakers did not rely solely on the optical characteristics of the 8mm ultra wide-angle lens,[14] and instead complemented the look they crafted with other techniques to create an appropriately disturbing moment.

Harry Potter and the Chamber of Secrets, Chris Columbus, Director; Roger Pratt, Cinematographer, 2002

Anamorphic lenses are designed to squeeze images along the x-axis, so that the entire film negative area or the active portion of a digital sensor can record an image that can be "de-squeezed" afterwards, either during projection or post-production (details of the anamorphic format can be found on page 47). These lenses are intended to be mounted with their concave front element vertically aligned to work properly, because in any other position (even if off by just a few degrees) the result will be an image that is noticeably slanted even after it is "de-squeezed". Some filmmakers, however, choose to purposely mount these lenses incorrectly, and use the abnormally slanted images to visualize a character's extreme physical or psychological state, often in scenes where someone is under the effects of psychoactive drugs, intense physical pain, or under the influence of another character or entity (via natural or supernatural means). The unusual look of this effect can be made even more dramatic by adding a dynamic aspect to the distortion, so that it fluidly changes direction as a shot progresses (done simply by manually rotating the anamorphic lens or anamorphic filter while shooting), making the image look as if it were being reflected on a funhouse mirror. The effect can be compounded by incorporating camera movement (especially when executed along the z-axis), zooming in or out, by using a tilt-shift lens, or all of these simultaneously. When using this dynamic form of anamorphic distortion, it is important to avoid allowing the lens to even momentarily align to its correct vertical position, or else the image will suddenly look undistorted in the middle of a shot.

An interesting example of this technique can be seen in Chris Columbus' *Harry Potter and the Chamber of Secrets*, the second installment of the series based on the Harry Potter books by J.K. Rowling. Set during Harry's second year at Hogwarts, the story follows the chaos that erupts when it is discovered that someone has opened the "chamber of secrets", freeing a monster with the power to petrify those with an "impure" bloodline. After Harry is unjustly accused of having opened the chamber, he decides to investigate who the real culprit is with the help of an enchanted diary that answers questions written on it. When he discovers that Ginny (Bonnie Wright) was taken into the chamber, he sets out to rescue her, but finds her unconscious and guarded by Tom Riddle, the writer of the diary, who eventually reveals himself as Harry's nemesis, Lord Voldemort. In the scene that follows, Riddle confesses he manipulated Ginny into opening the chamber of secrets through the diary, shown in a flashback that uses a special anamorphic lens attachment (known as a "mesmerizer" lens) with a geared ring that allows it to rotate with a follow focus attachment. The resulting images (left page, top and bottom frames) are not only extremely distorted, but their distortion stretches and shifts in different directions within every shot, giving them a surreal and dreamlike feel. The use of the anamorphic attachment in this scene is doubly appropriate, because it visualizes not only Ginny's trance-like behavior while she is under Riddle's spell, but also reflects the visual incongruity of seeing a trusted, innocent character being responsible for unleashing a deadly evil.

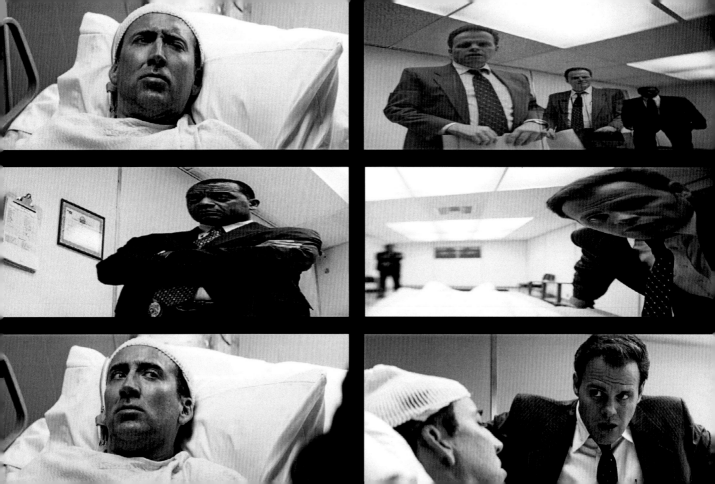

disorientation

The extreme stretching of the image achieved by mounting anamorphic lenses improperly (as seen in the previous section) can be combined with framing, editing, sound design, and any other techniques to amplify the overall effect of the distortion, providing a unique way to visualize a character's severe physical and/or psychological impairment. When combining techniques in this manner, it is important they are implemented in ways that complement one another and the general idea they are expressing. For instance, if the aim is to communicate that someone is experiencing distress, anamorphic distortion could be paired with unbalanced compositions, or canted angles, or any other cinematic visual convention that can signify something unusual or strange is happening. If, however, balanced compositions or otherwise conventionally framed shots were used instead, the impact of the anamorphic distortion would be diluted, and may even be misunderstood as a technical error and not an intended aesthetic choice.

A particularly effective illustration of this concept can be seen in director Ridley Scott's dark comedy *Matchstick Men*, when Roy Waller (Nicolas Cage), a con artist who suffers from Tourette syndrome and an array of obsessive compulsive behaviors, wakes up in a hospital bed after getting knocked out by one of his victims. As he gradually regains consciousness (left page, top left frame), he is confronted by two men who appear to be police detectives (Tim Kelleher and Nigel Gibbs) whom he has trouble seeing and hearing properly because of a head injury. This physical impairment is visualized by combining the extreme distortion of an improperly mounted anamorphic lens that stretches the image horizontally (middle left) with a wide-angle tilt-shift lens that overtly distorts perspective and restricts the plane of focus to the right side of the frame (middle right). These visual manipulations are further enhanced with a series of random dissolves and jump cuts that make one of the detectives suddenly appear in two areas of the room simultaneously (top right). Additionally, this scene incorporates several shifts of narrative perspective, alternating between distortion-free shots of Roy (top left, bottom left), and heavily distorted subjective shots of the detectives addressing the camera as if it were Roy (top right, middle right). These perspective shifts force the audience to constantly reassess how to interpret what they see and hear in this scene, at times as passive observers (when distortion-free shots are shown) and others as active participants (when subjective shots are used), adding a sense of disorientation that parallels Roy's physical impairment. The soundtrack is also distorted to complement the visualization of Roy's condition, featuring constantly shifting levels of reverb and sporadic instances of asynchronous dialogue that at times repeat lines spoken by the detective questioning him (echoing the unnatural doubling of his image). As Roy eventually manages to regain partial control of his senses, the visual and aural manipulations are interrupted and the narrative perspective remains objective, confirming they were motivated by his head injury (bottom right); this moment also provides a sharp visual contrast to the distortions used previously, amplifying their overall effect.

There Will Be Blood. *Paul Thomas Anderson, Director; Robert Elswit, Cinematographer. 2007.*

INTANGIBLES

Filmmakers need to be artists as well as technicians; they must know not only how their tools work, but also how to use them creatively to produce expressive images that serve a story and its themes. The basic technical characteristics of a lens are fairly easy to understand and control, but there are other, more subtle aspects that are unique to each lens that can also be instrumental in the creation of a look, like color bias, sharpness, flare structure, and vignetting profiles, among others; these intangible qualities give each lens an individual character, an "optical personality". Based on these intangibles, a cinematographer could choose a set of vintage glass over state-of-the-art lenses because of the look of the flares they produce, or because of the shape of their bokeh. Exploiting these intangible lens features often involves conducting extensive shooting tests, which can include using various lighting styles, production and/or distribution formats, weather conditions, filtration, postproduction processes, and even lens modifications (removing or adding elements by deconstructing a lens). Sometimes, this approach can lead to choosing lenses considered optically inferior and even defective, because they can produce looks modern lenses simply cannot replicate. Thanks to the DSLR revolution, a new generation of filmmakers shooting with interchangeable lenses are exploring the narrative potential of these intangible optical characteristics, reviving interest in vintage glass ranging from 1960s soviet-era still photography lenses, to retrofitted anamorphic attachments originally meant for movie theater projectors.

Director Paul Thomas Anderson and his long time collaborator, cinematographer Robert Elswit, devised a unique look for *There Will Be Blood*, Anderson's loose adaptation of Upton Sinclair's novel, *Oil!* Set during the California oil boom at the end of the 19th century, the story follows Daniel Plainview's (Daniel Day-Lewis) ruthless rise to power from mining silver to oil tycoon. Anderson, a director whose attention to detail and carefully crafted visuals has been compared to Stanley Kubrick's, has a predilection for the aesthetics of anamorphic lenses. This led him to use a combination of three different series of specially modified sets of Panavision anamorphics, and two Panavision spherical lenses with 40-year-old optics modified to make them anamorphic. Elswit used each of these lenses depending on the type of scenes being shot and the unique looks they could produce after they were modified (by swapping some elements and removing anti-reflective coatings to produce more organic-looking flares); one series of lenses was used exclusively for shooting interior scenes, another for exteriors, and a third for night sequences. Anderson also used a 43mm lens that was part of a Pathé vintage movie camera from 1910, which also had to be modified for anamorphic use.[15] This particular lens produced a "vintage" look, with lower contrast, noticeable vignetting, decreased sharpness, overt chromatic aberrations, and desaturated colors; while these optical shortcomings would be considered unacceptable by most filmmakers, they imbued the selected handful of shots in which this lens was used with a semblance of historical authenticity that would have been impossible to produce with a modern lens. Perhaps the best example of its use happens early in the film, in a shot that shows Daniel on a train with the baby he adopted after the accidental death of a worker (left page). Although it features noticeable optical distortion, prominent chromatic aberrations, and an overall lack of contrast, it nevertheless remains one of the most engaging and memorable images of the film.

Barry Lyndon. *Stanley Kubrick, Director; John Alcott, Cinematographer. 1975.*

naturalism

Given a choice, most filmmakers prefer to shoot with fast lenses, not just because they tend to produce higher quality images, but also because their wider maximum apertures allow working with lower light levels whether shooting exterior or interior scenes. However, although optical design and manufacturing technologies continue to improve, lenses have not become significantly faster than they have been for decades; this is in part due to inherent design limitations (the fastest theoretical lens speed is $f/0.5$) as well as practical considerations (even marginally faster lenses would be much larger, heavier, and cost considerably more). While faster lenses are out of reach, advancements in CMOS sensor technology have greatly increased low-light sensitivity while managing to keep noise within acceptable levels, making it feasible to shoot under very low light conditions. Shooting with ISO settings in the thousands and even tens of thousands while producing usable images is now a reality; for instance, the Sony A7s II, a mirrorless full-frame camera, can reach a staggering 409,600 ISO. This leap in low-light sensitivity, coupled with fast lenses that allow shooting at lower ISO settings to further minimize noise, are unleashing the expressive potential of shooting in extremely low-light conditions, letting filmmakers use virtually any available light as a main illuminating source. For the first time in the history of cinema it is possible for almost anyone to shoot night exterior scenes without the need of expensive, powerful movie lights, or to show a night sky with visible stars in the background of a shot while shooting at standard frame rates.

Almost 40 years ago, director Stanley Kubrick explored the expressive possibilities of shooting with natural light in *Barry Lyndon*, the story of a modest Irish rogue (Ryan O'Neal) who achieves wealth but ultimately squanders his chances of obtaining what he desires most: a title and the social status that comes with it. This film still occupies a unique place in the history of movies as the first major motion picture to use the fastest lens ever created, a customized Carl Zeiss Planar 50mm designed for NASA's Apollo missions, with a mind-blowing maximum aperture of $f/0.7$.[16] The fantastic speed of this lens, meant to capture images of the dark side of the Moon, allowed Kubrick and his cinematographer John Alcott to shoot night interiors using only candlelight, accurately recreating what these nocturnal environments looked like in the 18th century. Using the fastest lens ever made created some complications: the depth of field at the widest aperture was extremely shallow, severely limiting the blocking of actors, as shown in a scene where Redmond Barry (left page, top frame), impersonating a British officer, seduces a German peasant girl (Diana Körner). The lens also lacked sharpness, even in wider shots where the camera was relatively far from subjects (bottom left, right). Nonetheless, the air of historical authenticity created by using mostly natural light, coupled with a meticulous attention to detail in art direction and shot compositions inspired by paintings of the time, make watching *Barry Lyndon* a unique cinematic experience, and illustrate how any lens characteristic has the potential to help produce expressive, eloquent images that reflect a director's vision.

authenticity

Choosing a lens is the first step in a process that ends with a recorded image, and plays a crucial part in the final look of a film. However, it is just one of many factors that determines the way images look on a screen. Experienced cinematographers understand they have to know exactly how every step involved in the image creation process can affect the final product, from how a particular codec will render minute details in an actor's costume, to the way a given format will respond to over and underexposure, and anything in between. This is why it is common practice to shoot tests for formats, lighting, lenses, make-up, and so on, as required by the unique overall aesthetic, technical specifications, and workflow of a project. This kind of testing is even more important when a visual strategy incorporates unconventional or experimental techniques that deviate from standard practices, for instance, when trying out unusual combinations of formats, lenses, and postproduction processes.

When cinematographer Ellen Kuras devised the look for Ted Demme's *Blow*, the story of George Jung (Johnny Depp), an incredibly successful cocaine smuggler, she decided to give each time period covered in the film (1950s to 1990s) its own distinct visual style, based on key image references from each decade. Her visual strategy included using different film stocks, lighting styles, lab processes, color palettes, filtration, camera movement language, and even different lenses for each section of the film.[17] This approach required a tremendous amount of research on the cultural iconography of each time period, as well as the filmmaking technologies available in each decade (for instance, cam-era moves for scenes set in the 1950s and 1960s were done with a dolly instead of a Steadicam, which had not yet been invented at that time). Extensive tests were performed to gauge the effect of a number of film stocks and lab processing combinations, but perhaps the most brilliant decision she made had to do with lenses. While Kuras wanted each period to have a unique look, she did not want the audience to be distracted from the story by extreme visual changes. In an inspired move, she opted to use old anamorphic lenses instead of their optically superior contemporary versions for scenes that took place in the 1960s and 1970s, specifically early C and E series Panavision anamorphic primes (circa 1970s-1980s) ranging from 30mm to 800mm. The C series is a particularly interesting choice, because they have an uncoated, more organic look that CAD-engineered lenses generally lack, and produce what some would consider an inferior quality image when compared to modern lenses equipped with the latest anti–reflective coatings. These older lenses also produce more visible flares, and flatter, lower contrast images. These technical shortcomings would be considered unacceptable by most filmmakers, but they were ideal to emulate the look of iconic films from these decades after pairing them with carefully selected film stocks and postproduction processes, giving each of these sections its own distinctive visual style. While it would have been possible to mimic these looks through traditional photochemical color correction or digital means, they would have lacked the unique, unquantifiable optical characteristics that only lenses from these periods can produce.

The Assassination of Jesse James by the Coward Robert Ford. Andrew Dominik. Director: Roger Deakins, Cinematographer. 2007

similitude

An art form cannot evolve without artists who are willing to experiment, subvert conventions, and push boundaries. However, relatively few commercial filmmakers dare to try out new, bold techniques, especially if they impact the integrity of the image, which is usually expected to remain technically flawless. This is largely due to the economic realities associated with the astronomical production and marketing costs of major motion pictures, which tend to discourage any kind of extreme formal experimentation. Fortunately, there are still some established directors and cinematographers who continue to explore new ways to create expressive images to tell a story, at times even embracing an imperfect aesthetic created through the radical modification of the lenses they use.

An example of this kind of experimentation can be seen in the unique look created for certain shots in director Andrew Dominik's *The Assassination of Jesse James by the Coward Robert Ford*, an adaptation of Ron Hansen's novel that details the events leading to the death of Jesse James (Brad Pitt) and the complicated relationship he had with the man who idolized him but would eventually murder him, Robert Ford (Casey Affleck). This revisionist western features several key transitional scenes that include shots with a "tilt-shift" look, with distinct areas of blurriness toward the edges of the frame. Upon closer inspection, however, it becomes clear that a tilt-shift lens could not have been used in these particular shots (although it was used on others), because of the presence of pronounced color diffraction effects, image warping, and strong vignetting in the blurry ar-

eas of the frame. Cinematographer Roger Deakins achieved this unique look by creating a new kind of specialized lenses, nicknamed the "Deakinizers". Their unusual optical characteristics were obtained by removing the front element of a 9.8mm Kinoptik lens in some cases, and by adding elements from vintage wide-angle lenses to ARRI macros in others.[18] The concept behind these specialized lenses was to emulate the look of vintage glass used in early photographs Dominik selected for key visual references. Lenses from this era commonly produced images with overt vignetting, and exhibited a strong field curvature (an inability to focus an image over the entirety of the film plane, producing noticeable blurriness toward the frame edges). The Deakinizer shots (left page) effectively replicate the look of early archival photography from the Old West, imbuing these moments with a dreamlike, evocative, and historical quality. This "vintage aesthetic" is complemented by the use of the bleach bypass process (a photochemical postproduction technique that increases contrast and desaturates colors), which gives the film's color palette a slightly faded look, and also by the use of an omniscient, off-screen narrator speaking in past tense, who routinely provides insights into what characters are thinking as well as related historical tidbits, delivered in a style strongly reminiscent of a Ken Burns' documentary (particularly the series he produced on the American West). These choices make the overt stylization produced by the Deakinizer lenses feel organic to the mood, tone, and visual style of the film, helping to create a bold character study in this postmodernist reinterpretation of the classic western.

spontaneity

While it is important to know how the technical aspects of a lens can be manipulated to achieve a certain look, it is equally important to understand the less obvious ways our lens choices can affect the way we tell a story. Focal length, for instance, can have an unintended effect on performance, because of the way it determines camera placement once a shot size is selected (shooting a medium shot with a wide-angle lens, for instance, requires the camera to be much closer to a subject than the same shot taken with a telephoto lens). Although experienced actors are used to ignoring the presence of crew and equipment, they can sometimes be distracted by them, affecting their concentration and ability to be "in the moment". Knowing this, a director could, for instance, purposely choose long focal lengths when shooting a particularly demanding scene, so that camera and crew could be as far (and as unobtrusive) as possible from them. Focal length choice could even be part of a directing strategy – using zoom lenses and long camera to subject distances can keep actors unaware of the shot size being taken at any point during a scene, preventing them from modulating their performance depending on whether they are in a tight or a wide shot (for instance, by delivering broader physical gestures in long shots and more subtle facial expressions in close-ups). This technique can also be helpful when working with non-actors or when it is necessary to completely conceal the presence of a film crew (as used by director Yimou Zhang in selected scenes of *The Story of Qiu Ju*, examined on page 57), one of the reasons it is popular with documentary film-makers.

Director Jem Cohen's contemplative film *Museum Hours*, the story of the friendship that develops between Johann (Bobby Sommer), a Viennese museum guard, and Anne (Mary Margaret O'Hara), a Canadian woman visiting Austria to tend to a seriously ill relative (left page, top left frame), deftly uses telephoto lenses to document slices of everyday life that blur the line between fiction and non-fiction. As Johann helps Anne deal with her emergency, they end up exploring the museum and Vienna together, ruminating about their jobs, the meaning of the artworks, and their lives in the process. The film includes several detours from this main story, including unstaged footage of Vienna's Kunsthistorisches Museum visitors (middle right, left), an art historian's (Ela Piplits) insightful lecture on a painting by Pieter Bruegel the Elder that reveals a documentary dimension to his work (top right), and seemingly random street scenes showing everyday activities that take on an artistic significance as the story progresses (bottom left). Many of these moments are shot with long telephoto lenses that allowed the camera to be far from the action, giving these scenes a spontaneous, observational quality normally associated with documentaries. At times, even scenes that feature Anne and Johann are shot from afar without the knowledge of the people around them (bottom right), perfectly blending the real with the staged. The narrative importance of capturing these partially unscripted moments with the help of telephoto lenses is revealed gradually, as the film establishes the value of finding artistic meaning and even transcendent beauty in common, everyday objects, places, actions, and people.

Only God Forgives, Nicolas Winding Refn, Director; Larry Smith, Cinematographer, 2013

texture

Before the advent of high dynamic range professional HD digital formats, filmmakers only had a few film stocks to choose from when shooting a movie; of these, only Kodak remains, thanks to a handful of influential Hollywood directors who dislike the "digital look", and believe that film is still the gold standard in terms of resolution and dynamic range. These filmmakers also prefer the "texture" of film, which they feel digital formats simply cannot replicate. Complaints about the "video look" of professional digital formats are centered on its "hardness" and "coldness"; this aesthetic is the result of a combination of factors, from the idiosyncracies of how sensors react to light and render color, to the encoding algorithms and bit depth of the format. Things get even more complicated when dealing with DSLRs, mirrorless, and semi-professional video cameras, because they often use their own proprietary codecs, designed to complement their unique hardware and software, resulting in each producing their own distinctive version of the "digital look". Additionally, ISO choice can also have a significant impact on the final look of images, especially when it deviates from a camera's "native" ISO (the setting that optimizes dynamic range, detail, and produces the lowest noise, analogous to a lens' sweet spot). The shift to high-end digital video formats has effectively forced filmmakers to become knowledgeable of all the technical intricacies of their cameras, formats, and workflows to have full control over the look of the images they produce; because of this, it is more important than ever to understand how lens choices will complement the specific digital idiosyncrasies of the camera you intend to use.

While preparing to shoot his first digital feature film, Nicolas Winding Refn's phantasmagoric *Only God Forgives*, cinematographer Larry Smith wanted to conduct extensive shooting tests to get acquainted with the various looks and formats of the cameras he chose for the production (the ARRI ALEXA shooting in ProRes 4:4:4:4 Log C, and the Red Epic shooting in 5K); unfortunately, budgetary constraints resulted in getting the cameras only a few days before production began. This setback was especially troubling because of the highly stylized aesthetic that was part of the visual strategy for this film, which relied heavily on using practical neon lights, a vivid color palette, and plenty of night scenes (left page). Smith made one key decision from the onset, however: he would use Cooke S4 lenses to counteract the "hard, fierce, and unforgiving" digital look.[19] Among many professional cinematographers, Zeiss and Cooke are considered among the best cinema lenses available, but they are also seen as having fundamentally different visual qualities: Zeiss lenses are thought to be a bit cold and almost "clinically" sharp, while Cooke glass is perceived as being warmer, producing a more organic, slightly softer look. While it is difficult to quantify these differences and almost impossible to notice them on smaller screens, they can result in noticeably different looks when projected in a movie theater setting. Beyond the arrestingly beautiful cinematography of *Only God Forgives*, it also exemplifies what is rapidly becoming a new visual standard in mainstream filmmaking that falls somewhere between a digital and a film look, due in part to a thoughtful pairing of lenses and digital formats.

Tangerine, Sean Baker. Director: Sean Baker, Radium Cheung, Cinematographers, 2015.

uniqueness

It is sometimes easy to get caught up with the notion that we need to have the most advanced and expensive lenses we can afford if we want to create exceptional images for a film. While recent improvements in the resolution, dynamic range, and low-light sensitivity of even lower priced DSLRs and mirrorless cameras are making it possible for almost anyone to produce polished, professional-looking video, the effectiveness of these tools to tell compelling stories is always contingent on the user's ability to understand and exploit the inherent advantages and disadvantages they offer a particular project. This concept also applies to lenses; having a lens worth thousands of dollars on your camera is not as important as knowing how any lens you have access to, regardless of its cost or quality, can be used to control the images you create so they expressively reflect the ideas and themes of your film.

This principle is beautifully illustrated in Sean Baker's film *Tangerine*, a compassionate, endearing portrait of two transgender L.A. sex workers, Sin-Dee Rella (Kitana Kiki Rodriguez) and Alexandra (Mya Taylor), as their friendship is tested one Christmas Eve. The microbudget film was shot entirely on an iPhone 5s, using only a tiny anamorphic lens attachment by Moondog Labs that allowed capturing a wide-screen image using the phone's entire sensor, and FiLMiC Pro, an app that provides access to higher bit rate video at 24 frames per second and manual aperture, color temperature, and focusing.[20] The resulting look is a hybrid of some aspects of the anamorphic format (including anamorphic lens flares and a 2.39:1 aspect ratio), and the deep depth of field commonly associated with smartphone video (the iPhone 5s has an *f*/2.2 lens with a focal length of only 4.1mm, equivalent to roughly 33mm in the 35mm format). Cinematographers Sean Baker and Radium Cheung use these distinctive qualities to create a unique, original visual style that perfectly complements the unconventional nature of the story, the characters, the setting, and the subculture the film explores. The deep depth of field, for instance, is utilized to showcase every detail of the Santa Monica Boulevard area where much of the action takes place (an unofficial red light district for transgender sex workers), in shots that keep everything in sharp focus (left page, top left, right); it is also complemented with shot compositions that emphasize the depth of the frame, used variously to stylize the look of a location's architecture (middle left), and to visualize relationship dynamics between characters (middle right). Likewise, the extra wide aspect ratio produced by the anamorphic attachment is often used to reflect characters' psychological and emotional states through the expressive use of negative space (bottom left, right). Shooting with smartphones instead of large, heavy professional camera rigs also allowed the filmmakers to easily incorporate a lot of camera movement while remaining largely unnoticed by passersby, adding a gritty, almost documentary quality that would not have been possible otherwise. *Tangerine*'s unique cinematography demonstrates that an understanding of both the narrative and technical capabilities of lenses can unleash their full expressive potential, whether you are working with glass worth tens of thousands of dollars or the tiny lens of a smartphone.

references

1   Lanthier, Joseph Jon. "Interview: Shane Carruth Talks *Upstream Color*." *Slant Magazine*, Slant Magazine, 4 Apr. 2013, https://www.slantmagazine.com/film/interview-shane-carruth/. Accessed March 23, 2019.

2   Gomez-Rejon, Alfonso. Audio commentary. *Me & Earl and the Dying Girl*, Dir. Alfonso Gomez-Rejon. Indian Paintbrush, 2015. BluRay.

3   Romanek, Mark. Anatomy of a scene/cinematography special feature. *One Hour Photo*, Dir. Mark Romanek. Fox Searchlight Pictures, 2002. DVD.

4   Hannaford, Alex. "25 Years of 'Stand by Me'." *The Telegraph*. Telegraph Media Group, 13 June 2011, https://www.telegraph.co.uk/culture/books/8566133/25-years-of-Stand-by-Me.html. Accessed March 23, 2019.

5   Magid, Ron. "In Search of the David Lean Lens." *American Cinematographer*, Apr. 1989, pp. 95-98.

6   Truffaut, François, et al. Hitchcock / by François Truffaut; with the Collaboration of Helen G. Scott. Simon and Schuster, 1983, p.290.

7   Goldman, Michael. "Left for Dead." *American Cinematographer*, Jan. 2016, pp. 51-52.

8   Ballinger, Alexander. *New Cinematographers*. Harper Design International, 2004, p.182.

9   Buder, Emily. "How 'Beautiful Camera Mistakes' Brought van Gogh to the Screen Courtesy of DP Benoît Delhomme." *No Film School*. Nonetwork LLC., Nov. 14, 2018, https://nofilmschool.com/2018/11/benoît-delhomme-eternitys-gate. Accessed March 23, 2019.

10 Ballinger, Alexander. *New Cinematographers*. Harper Design International, 2004, p. 27.

11 Pizzello, Stephen. "Artistry and the 'Happy Accident'." *Theasc.com*. The American Society of Cinematographers, May 2003, https://theasc.com/magazine/may03/cover/index.html. Accessed March 23, 2019.

12 Ballinger, Alexander. *New Cinematographers*. Harper Design International, 2004, pp.118-121.

13 Bergery, Benjamin. "Cinematic Impressionism." *American Cinematographer*, Dec. 2004, p. 61.

14 Libatique, Matthew. Audio commentary. *Requiem for a Dream*, Dir. Darren Aronofsky. Artisan Entertainment, 2000. BluRay.

15 Pizzello, Stephen. "Blood for Oil." *American Cinematographer*, Jan. 2008, pp. 39-42.

16 Lightman, Herb A. "Photographing Stanley Kubrick's Barry Lyndon." *American Cinematographer*, March 1976, pp. 338-340.

17 Goodridge, Mike, and Grierson, Tim. *Cinematography*. Focal Press, 2012, p. 143.

18 Pizzello, Stephen and K. Bosley, Rachael. "Western Destinies." *American Cinematographer*, Oct. 2007, p. 37.

19 Pizzello, Stephen. "Bangkok Dangerous." *American Cinematographer*, Sept. 2013, p. 56.

20 Thomson, Patricia. "Sundance 2015: Inspiring Indies." *Theasc.com*. The American Society of Cinematographers, Feb. 2015, https://theasc.com/ac_magazine/February2015/Sundance2015/page5.html. Accessed March 23, 2019.

filmography

2001: A Space Odyssey. Dir. Stanley Kubrick. Metro-Goldwyn-Mayer, 1968.

Adaptation. Dir. Spike Jonze. Propaganda Films, 2002.

Age of Uprising: The Legend of Michael Kohlhaas. Dir. Arnaud des Pallières. Les Films d'Ici, *2013*.

Amélie. Dir. Jean-Pierre Jeunet. Claudie Ossard Productions, 2001.

The Assassination of Jesse James by the Coward Robert Ford. Dir. Andrew Dominik. Warner Bros., 2007.

At Eternity's Gate. Dir. Julian Schnabel. Riverstone Pictures, 2018.

Bad Boys II. Dir. Michael Bay. Don Simpson/Jerry Bruckheimer Films, 2003.

Barry Lyndon. Dir. Stanley Kubrick. Warner Bros., 1975.

Barton Fink. Dirs. Joel Coen, Ethan Coen. Working Title Films, 1991.

Batman Begins. Dir. Christopher Nolan. Warner Bros., 2005.

The Best Years of Our Lives. Dir. William Wyler. Samuel Goldwyn Company, 1946.

Blow. Dir. Ted Demme. New Line Cinema, 2001.

Capote. Dir. Bennett Miller. Sony Pictures Classics, 2005.

Captain Phillips. Dir. Paul Greengrass. Scott Rudin Productions, 2013.

Citizen Kane. Dir. Orson Welles. RKO Radio Pictures, 1941.

A Clockwork Orange. Dir. Stanley Kubrick. Warner Bros., 1971.

Close Encounters of the Third Kind. Dir. Steven Spielberg. Columbia Pictures Corporation, 1977.

The Constant Gardener. Dir. Fernando Meirelles. Focus Features, 2005.

Cool Hand Luke. Dir. Stuart Rosenberg. Jalem Productions, 1967.

The Departed. Dir. Martin Scorsese. Warner Bros., 2006.

The Descent. Dir. Neil Marshall. Celador Films, 2005.

The Diving Bell and the Butterfly. Dir. Julian Schnabel. Pathé Renn Productions, 2007.

Django Unchained. Dir. Quentin Tarantino. The Weinstein Company, 2012.

Dolores Claiborne. Dir. Taylor Hackford. Castle Rock Entertainment, 1995.

The Duellists. Dir. Ridley Scott. Paramount Pictures, 1977.

Easy Rider. Dir. Dennis Hopper. Pando Company Inc., 1969.

Election. Dir. Alexander Payne. MTV Films, 1999.

Electronic Labyrinth THX 1138 4EB. Dir. George Lucas. University of Southern California (USC), 1967.

Elephant. Dir. Gus Van Sant. Fine Line Features, 2003.

Elizabeth. Dir. Shekhar Kapur. Working Title Films, 1998.

Far from the Madding Crowd. Dir. Thomas Vinterberg. BBC Films, 2015.

The Favourite. Dir. Yorgos Lanthimos. Element Pictures, 2018.

Fear and Loathing in Las Vegas. Dir. Terry Gilliam. Universal Pictures, 1998.

The Girl with the Dragon Tattoo. Dir. David Fincher. Columbia Pictures, 2011.

The Good, the Bad and the Ugly. Dir. Sergio Leone. Produzioni Europee Associati, 1966.

Harold and Maude. Dir. Hal Ashby. Paramount Pictures, 1971.

Harry Potter and the Chamber of Secrets. Dir. Chris Columbus. Warner Bros., 2002.

Heat. Dir. Michael Mann. Warner Bros.,1995.

The Hobbit: An Unexpected Journey. Dir. Peter Jackson. WingNut Films, 2012.

The Innocents. Dir. Jack Clayton. Twentieth Century Fox Film Corporation, 1961.

K–PAX. Dir. Iain Softley. Intermedia Films, 2001.

Kagemusha. Dir. Akira Kurosawa. Kurosawa Production Co., 1980.

The King's Speech. Dir. Tom Hooper. The Weinstein Company, 2010.

Kung Fu Hustle. Dir. Stephen Chow. Columbia Pictures Film Production Asia, 2004.

Lawrence of Arabia. Dir. David Lean. Horizon Pictures, 1962.

Lourdes. Dir. Jessica Hausner. ARTE, 2009.

The Machinist. Dir. Brad Anderson. Castelao Producciones, 2004.

Malcolm X. Dir. Spike Lee. 40 Acres & A Mule Filmworks, 1992.

Matchstick Men. Dir. Ridley Scott. Warner Bros., 2003.

Me and Earl and the Dying Girl. Dir. Alfonso Gomez-Rejon. Indian Paintbrush, 2015.

Midnight Cowboy. Dir. John Schlesinger. Jerome Hellman Productions, 1969.

Mission: Impossible. Dir. Brian De Palma. Paramount Pictures, 1996.

Mommy. Dir. Xavier Dolan. Société de Développement des Enterprises Culturelles, 2014.

Museum Hours. Dir. Jem Cohen. Little Magnet Films, 2012.

Notes on a Scandal. Dir. Richard Eyre. Fox Searchlight Pictures, 2006.

One Hour Photo. Dir. Mark Romanek. Fox Searchlight Pictures, 2002.

Only God Forgives. Dir. Nicolas Winding Refn. Space Rocket Nation, 2013.

The Possession of Hannah Grace. Dir. Diederik Van Rooijen. Screen Gems, 2018.

Primer. Dir. Shane Carruth. erbp, 2004.

Prisoners. Dir. Denis Villeneuve. Madhouse Entertainment, 2013.

The Program. Dir. Stephen Frears. Working Title Films, 2015.

Punch-Drunk Love. Dir. Paul Thomas Anderson. New Line Cinema, 2002.

Ran. Dir. Akira Kurosawa. Nippon Herald Films, 1985.

Rango. Dir. Gore Verbinski. Paramount Pictures, 2011.

Requiem for a Dream. Dir. Darren Aronofsky. Artisan Entertainment, 2000.

The Return. Dir. Andrey Zvyagintsev. Ren Film, 2003.

The Revenant. Dir. Alejandro G. Iñárritu. New Regency Pictures, 2015.

The Rules of the Game. Dir. Jean Renoir. Nouvelles Éditions de Films (NEF), 1939.

Rumble Fish. Dir. Francis Ford Coppola. Zoetrope Studios, 1983.

Run Lola Run. Dir. Tom Tykwer. Westdeutscher Rundfunk, 1998.

Schindler's List. Dir. Steven Spielberg. Amblin Entertainment, 1993.

Se7en. Dir. David Fincher. New Line Cinema, 1995.

Seven Samurai. Dir. Akira Kurosawa. Toho Company, 1954.

Sexy Beast. Dir. Jonathan Glazer. FilmFour, 2000.

Sideways. Dir. Alexander Payne. Fox Searchlight Pictures, 2004.

Stand by Me. Dir. Rob Reiner. Columbia Pictures Corporation, 1986.

Star Trek. Dir. J.J. Abrams. Paramount Pictures, 2009.

The Story of Qiu Ju. Dir. Yimou Zhang. Youth Film Studio of Beijing Film Academy, 1992.

Submarine. Dir. Richard Ayoade. Warp Films, 2010.

Sunshine. Dir. Danny Boyle. UK Film Council, 2007.

Tangerine. Dir. Sean Baker. Duplass Brothers Productions, 2015.

There Will Be Blood. Dir. Paul Thomas Anderson. Miramax, 2007.

Thérèse. Dir. Claude Miller. Les Films du 24, 2012.

THX 1138. Dir. George Lucas. American Zoetrope, 1971.

Tootsie. Dir. Sydney Pollack. Columbia Pictures Corporation, 1982.

The Tree of Life. Dir. Terrence Malick. Plan B Entertainment, 2011.

Upstream Color. Dir. Shane Carruth. erbp, 2013.

We Need to Talk About Kevin. Dir. Lynne Ramsay. UK Film Council, 2011.

image credits

Figure 2   Photo courtesy of ZEISS
Figure 11 (b)   Photo courtesy of Canon, Inc.
Figure 13   Photo courtesy of ZEISS
Figure 14   Photos courtesy of Canon, Inc.
Figure 17 (b)   Photo courtesy of Canon, Inc.
Figure 22   Screenshots courtesy of David Eubank - Thin Man Inc.
Figure 31   Photos courtesy of Canon, Inc.
Figure 33 (a)   Photo courtesy of Panavision
Figure 33 (b)   Photo courtesy of Cooke Optics Limited
Figure 35 (a)   Photo courtesy of Canon, Inc.
Figure 35 (b)   Photo courtesy of Canon, Inc.
Figure 35 (c)   Photo courtesy of Lensbaby

Original illustrations and photographs by Gustavo Mercado

index

Boldface indicates film titles. *Italicized* numbers indicate illustrations/film stills

T - #0158 - 181220 - C208 - 229/229/12 - PB - 9780415821315